A New Game Plan for Illinois

James D. Nowlan

Published by
Neltnor House
Chicago, Illinois

Published in the United States of America in 1989 by
Neltnor House
P.O. Box 64389
State of Illinois Center Station
Chicago, Illinois 60664-0389
Telephone: 312/649-9890

© 1989 by James D. Nowlan

Library of Congress Cataloging-in-Publication Data

Nowlan, James Dunlap, 1941-
  A new game plan for Illinois.

  Bibliography: p.
  Includes index.
  1. Electioneering--Illinois. 2. Illinois--Politics and government--1951- . I. Title.
JK5795.N677 1989   324.7'09773   89-9251
ISBN 0-9622680-0-3

Cover design by Patricia M. Bomher

Contents

Acknowledgements	vii
Dedication	ix
Introduction	1
1. The Changing Faces of Illinois	5
2. Sorting Things Out—Citizen, Community, and Government	19
3. Goals for Illinois	33
4. Productivity and Education	41
5. Economic Development	57
6. To Help Every Poor Child	77
7. Images and Realities—the Creative Arts, Our Natural Resources, and Rural Illinois	93
8. Budgeting and Taxing for a New Game Plan	111
9. Managing the State	127
10. Leadership and Change	145
11. Beyond the Margins of Our Mediocrity—A Summary Essay	163
Notes on Important Sources	167
Bibliography	169
Index	181

Acknowledgements

Several friends whom I respect for their understanding of Illinois issues took of their valuable time to read and comment on all or parts of the text. This fact represents neither endorsement nor agreement with any of the proposals made in the pages that follow.

They are Robert G. Cronson, Auditor General of Illinois; Donald Fouts, president of the Federation of Independent Illinois Colleges and Universities; Samuel K. Gove, professor and director emeritus of the Institute of Government and Public Affairs at the University of Illinois; Sister Julia Huiskamp, of Catholic Urban Programs of East St. Louis.

And Jim Krohe, associate editor of *Illinois Times*; Charles Levesque, director of community development for the Illinois Community Action Agency; Donald Neltnor, executive vice president of the City Club of Chicago; Connie Revell, vice president of the Federation of Independent Illinois Colleges and Universities; Jerry Stermer, president of Voices for Illinois Children, and Douglas Whitley, president of the Taxpayers' Federation of Illinois. Their suggestions, corrections, and criticisms saved me from numerous errors of fact and interpretation.

Howard A. Wilson, professor emeritus of English at Knox College, provided editorial suggestions that clarify the text throughout. Frances Dixon Bond of Urbana contributed valuable editorial guidance on early drafts of several sections of the book.

Robert J. R. Follett, Charles P. Wolff, and Richard J. Dennis have been supportive throughout. John Strassburger, dean of Knox College, has been generous in providing research support. Christopher Everson, my research assistant, has been helpful in double-checking citations and sources. Kelly Shaw-Barnes, my administrative assistant, is immensely capable. Her work in helping me prepare the manuscript—as computer specialist, editor, gadfly—has been of great value.

Bill Campbell drew the editorial cartoons that break up my ponderous prose. The artwork is as timely and telling in 1989 as when the cartoons were first published a decade ago.

My thanks go to all of them. Errors go solely to me.

James D. Nowlan
Galesburg, Illinois
February 22, 1989

Dedication

I first met Bill Campbell in the early 1970s in the DTL (Downtown Lounge), a Galesburg, Illinois watering hole popular then with the courthouse crowd, Knox College students, and an assortment of colorful reprobates like the local bookies. Campbell (as he is called) was a reporter for the Galesburg *Register-Mail* and there were stories to be found at the DTL. He was also addicted to the foosball table in the smoky back room.

Following several statewide newswriting awards, Campbell shifted from writing to drawing editorial cartoons. Soon his cartoons were being syndicated in 80 newspapers; he became Pulitzer Prize winner John Fischetti's regular backup at the Chicago *Daily News*, and in 1978 he won a national competition. His career was beginning to skyrocket.

In 1979 Campbell was in an auto accident that left him paralyzed from the neck down. Cartooning career over? Yes. Corpus limp? Yes. Spirit down? Hell no, never!

After a year in hospitals, Campbell moved back to the family farm in western Illinois. He taught himself to peck out newspaper columns on a computer, a pencil attached via a leather splint to the hand of the one arm he could move, and sometimes control. Campbell's columns are carried by 20 Illinois newspapers. They are required reading for thousands, especially for those who work in a factory or on the farm. Campbell gives voice to these readers, to their fears, opinions, hopes, dreams.

A former paratrooper, he writes with salty good humor. On politics, for example, he reflects that if A. Lincoln had observed our lawmakers haggling over the "Build Illinois" pork barrel projects, Abe would surely have insisted that our license plates proclaim ours as the "Land of Somebody Else."

Besides the thousands he reaches with his columns and books, Campbell motivates people directly. He regularly hosts a seminar for college credit that meets weekly to discuss issues in the U.S. Constitution. The students from Monmouth College gather in a circle with Campbell near his fireplace and carry on lively arguments with this college dropout about free speech, libel, creationism, and due process.

Yet I know the biggest lesson for these students is never mentioned—that for spirit, love of life, and a passion to convince people to be better than they thought they were, these students can't hold a candle to this guy who can't hold a candle.

This book is dedicated to my buddy Campbell.

Introduction

This book presents one man's platform for Illinois for the coming generation. I have several purposes. They are to:
* Stir you to react.
* Stir you to informed and active participation in the political process, if you have been on the sidelines.
* Frame the debate during the Illinois gubernatorial campaign of 1990 around fundamental problems and solutions, and away from the empty slogans that characterize most election contests.
* Challenge candidates to prepare and present their own platforms, so that they develop—while they still have the opportunity—a plan of what they want to accomplish and how they intend to go about it.

Once inside government there is neither the time nor the incentive to think and look ahead. There is today's insurance crisis to solve, prison disturbance to quell, natural disaster to ameliorate, protest group to placate, and political brush fire to dampen. The future is never more distant than the next election, which is always visible on the horizon. Why then would any practical politician look ahead?

In November-December 1976 I served on Illinois Governor-elect James R. Thompson's transition team that prepared for his accession to office. I recall going into the office of James Fletcher, who was to become Thompson's first deputy governor. "Fletch" was almost literally snowed under by piles of phone messages—more than 400 of them!—that he was trying to work through. Once in office the name of the game is catch up, not reflection, not anticipation.

Former North Carolina governor and present U.S. Senator

2 A NEW GAME PLAN FOR ILLINOIS

Terry Sanford once lamented, "There is no one in the governor's office whose only job is to gaze out the window and brood about the problems of the future." That still holds true in Illinois, based on my experiences over the past two decades as state legislator and aide to two governors.

State government in Illinois operates in the past, not the present, let alone the future. For example, education reform was not initiated in Illinois until 1985, more than a decade after pupil test scores had begun to decline, and indeed after scores had begun to rise once again.

In the early 1980s we engaged in frenetic efforts to create high tech economies on short order, along the lines of Silicon Valley and the Route 128 corridor in Massachusetts. What we fail to appreciate is that these success stories were rooted in the 1940s, when a relatively few creative and entrepreneurial men planted the seeds for growth that reached full bloom decades later.

Instead of looking down the pike a few years, we plod along and react late to long festering problems. We talk boldly and act meekly. For example, four years after we "reformed" education the state is providing early childhood education programs to only 11,000 of 112,000 3- and 4-year-olds at great risk of becoming tomorrow's dropouts, teen mothers, and prison inmates.

The so-called reforms never even addressed the fundamental issues of a longer school day and longer school year. We continue to operate our schools on the basis of a 19th Century farm growing season that allowed for 175-180 school days a year, while the Japanese send their children to school 240 days annually.

It is as if we are sleepwalking through our own slow, barely perceptible decline. I am reminded of the tale about frogs placed in a saucepan of cold water. If the temperature is raised oh-so-slowly the frogs will stay in the water until they boil to death, rather than jump out at some point to save themselves.

So I brood a bit in the essays that follow. I also prescribe. When I set out on this project I thought my most important contribution would be to present a list of policy proposals by which to address our problems. Yet I found that work had already been done. The National Governors' Association, the Urban League, and a score of think tanks have generated a

cornucopia of policy ideas and pilot projects. Unfortunately we seem incapable of moving beyond the relatively inexpensive pilot projects that affect a handful of people. Why? I think it is because:
* We have failed to focus on the issues that will define Illinois.
* We have not agreed on clear, measurable goals.
* There is a sense of futility that nothing we can do will make much difference anyway.

There are at least five issues that will define Illinois for the coming generation. Each will be discussed later. They are:

1. Education. Half the 65 public high schools in Chicago rank in the bottom one percent of all high schools in the U.S. on test scores. The math and science achievement test scores of our *best* Illinois students are barely at the average of test scores for all Japanese school children at the same grade levels.

2. The Underclass. I am told that half the boys living in the Cabrini-Green public housing project, located near Chicago's glistening Loop skyscrapers, will be dead or in prison by age 18. Nobody knows for sure, but the figures don't startle those who are familiar with the dark, scary world of "the projects." The level of our commitment to the children of the underclass will define for the world who we are and what we are about.

3. Perceptions. We lack clear positive pictures of ourselves and of our state, while the world at large tends to have outdated, negative pictures of Chicago, and none at all of Illinois.

4. Confidence. Nationally, trust and confidence in our governmental institutions to do the right thing have plummeted since 1960. In addition, in Illinois there is a strong sense of detached futility, as in "what can little ol' me do about our problems," and "nobody knows how to solve the problems of the poor and undereducated, so why throw more money at them?"

5. Community and Government. We have come to see big government as an abstract blob that is supposed to solve society's problems. Since governments take about one third of our income, that surely is enough to deal with any problems we have. No longer is government thought of as an extension of community, an instrument to assist community and citizens in meeting our obligations.

The platform that follows addresses these defining issues.

4 A NEW GAME PLAN FOR ILLINOIS

Chapter 1 sketches the rapidly changing faces of Illinois and evaluates how we stack up with other states and the world on basic social indicators. Chapters 2 and 3 attempt to clarify what it is we want to accomplish for our community of Illinois, and how we might reorganize and focus ourselves in order to do so. To assist in this, I propose clear, measurable goals for the coming generation.

Chapters 4 through 7 comprise my platform's policy proposals for achieving the goals. Several proposals might strike you as dramatic, even radical: foreign languages from early grammar school through high school, a required semester abroad for college students, and a program to speed up the depopulation of the ghettos of the underclass. I assure you, however, that the proposals are based on programs that other countries have required for years, or that we have implemented in other forms in the United States.

In Chapter 8 I tell you what the bills would be for my proposals and how we could tax ourselves more fairly to pay them. Chapter 9 draws upon my experience inside Illinois state government to recommend new approaches to managing this $22 billion enterprise, and in Chapter 10 I discuss leadership, ethics, and long-term thinking, elements that are critical to the fundamental change that I call for earlier.

For readers who compulsively turn to the back of new novels to find out how it all ends, I have provided a summary essay in Chapter 11 that tries to squeeze the essence out of my laboured text.

To spare you the distractions of footnotes, but to convince you I drew upon many sources more learned and thoughtful than am I, notes on important sources and a bibliography are gathered at the end of the book. Other than for newspaper reportage, works and authors cited in the text are to be found in the bibliography.

For skeptics who might dismiss my proposals and goals as utopian, I respond that each is already implemented and achieved and even bettered somewhere on earth. I am simply not willing to consign Illinois to anything less. I propose instead a new game plan for Illinois for your consideration.

Chapter 1

The Changing Faces of Illinois

Illinois has been called a political and economic microcosm of the nation. While this is a simplification, Illinois comprises great diversity that tends to reflect the nation as a whole. The state's northernmost latitude is close to that of Portsmouth, New Hampshire; the southernmost, near that of Portsmouth, Virginia.

Early settlers to the state came from both South and North. Census figures for 1880 showed that the southern half of the state had been settled largely by English and Scots stock via Virginia, Tennessee, and Kentucky, while the northern half had been populated by a mix of northern Europeans who were to be followed by central and southern Europeans, from Poland to Italy. In this century there has been major movement into the state by blacks, Hispanics, and Asians.

The cultural and regional diversity persists. The classic "southern" movie, *In the Heat of the Night*, featuring Sidney Poitier and Rod Steiger, was filmed almost entirely in the southern Illinois towns of Sparta and Chester, because they seemed to reflect a southern culture. Yet these towns are not even in deep southern Illinois. In my former state legislative district in central Illinois, I enjoyed drinking a beer now and then at the Latino-Americano Club in Rock Falls, the Flemish-American Club in Kewanee, and the Italian chicken-and-spaghetti taverns in Ladd and Dalzell. Chicago has the world's largest Polish population outside Warsaw and Krakow. You will often hear more Polish and Spanish than English spoken on the rapid transit trains that whisk you northwest from Chicago's Loop to O'Hare Airport.

"Illinois is the best bellweather state in America," says

6 A NEW GAME PLAN FOR ILLINOIS

pollster Peter Hart. "It is a state that has it all: north, south, urban, rural, black, white, Hispanic. What usually plays well nationally plays pretty well in Illinois." Illinois has contributed its electoral votes to every twentieth century president with the exception of Wilson in 1916 and Carter in 1976. Students of Illinois politics used to examine elections by dividing the state into Chicago and Downstate. Now Illinois is viewed as having three regions: Chicago, with 3 million people; the 5 1/2 counties that form a "collar" around Chicago, with 4.4 million, and the remaining 96 Downstate counties, with about 4.3 million.

Chicago remains strongly Democratic, though there is clear erosion of loyalty among ethnic whites; the collar counties are heavily Republican, and Downstate—often thought to be Republican—is balanced politically. As a result, Illinois has highly competitive statewide elections and a legislature in which party majorities are often razor-thin and control has often been divided, with Democrats controlling one house and Republicans the other.

Shared Values Yet Provincial Distrust

Caesar divided Gaul into several provinces, the better to govern it. We in Illinois seem to have divided ourselves into three regions, with opposite effect. We don't know one another well, from one region to the next. Metro Chicago residents generally take their weekend vacations in Wisconsin or Michigan, not downstate. Most of southern Illinois is closer to Memphis than to Chicago. Downstaters enjoy chartered bus trips to Wrigley Field and Comiskey Park for ball games, yet seldom stray more than a few feet from their rides home.

Collar county residents feel self-sufficient, with sprawling malls and increasing cultural amenities; many go for years without venturing into Chicago. In 1978 when I was managing the successful re-election campaign of then U.S. senator Charles Percy, I hosted our collar county volunteer coordinators for luncheon in the stately Walnut Room of Marshall Field's State Street store. "How often do you ladies come into the Loop?" I asked. "Oh, I never come in" and "This is the first time I've been in the Loop in years" were the typical responses.

Lack of understanding and distrust can often result from regional separation. This is not new. In the 1870s visitors in the

THE CHANGING FACES OF ILLINOIS 7

gallery of the Illinois House of Representatives were treated to raucous debates over whether to cede Chicago to Wisconsin or Indiana. In recent decades this distrust has generated efforts by each region to get its "fair share" of each major allocation, regardless of need. For example, in the early 1960s, when we were overbuilding public higher education, Chicago couldn't get $50 million to construct a campus of the University of Illinois unless Southern Illinois University got $25 million for a new campus at Edwardsville, near St. Louis. And when additional universities were put on the drawing boards a few years later, one had to be drawn for the suburbs, another for downstate. A case could be made for each university, but not for all of them.

In 1984 the Chicago public school system requested $22 million from the legislature to bail it out of a strike. The two other regions insisted on their "fair shares." As a result, $75 million was appropriated, something for all districts. These other districts were not on strike, had not budgeted for nor expected the windfall. Thus the strike in Chicago cost us more than three times the asking price.

8 A NEW GAME PLAN FOR ILLINOIS

In 1987 the Institute of Government of the University of Illinois conducted a lengthy survey of 2600 Illinois residents in an effort to examine regional differences. The findings confirm the distrust, but found remarkable similarities of attitudes across regions as to values, quality of life issues, and the role of government. A majority in each region felt that legislators from other regions sometimes oppose legislation that might benefit an area other than the one they represent.

The most negative views were held by non-Chicagoans toward Chicago. Half the respondents from outside Chicago believe that "Chicagoans neither care about the welfare of the rest of the state nor would they support a legislative program benefiting these other regions." Ironically another poll, taken by Market Opinion Research of Detroit in the early 1980s, found Chicagoans actually highly sympathetic to Illinois farmers, with two-thirds of Chicagoans indicating that farmers had too little political influence.

Clearly, we do not know one another well, and we are the poorer for it, I believe.

The Changing Faces of Illinois

Abraham Lincoln spoke of the need to know where we have been and whither we are tending, the better to know how to proceed. This is apt guidance for Illinois, for our state has been undergoing a dramatic, largely unnoticed transformation in recent years. Since 1970 the Illinois population has been growing slowly, by 2.8 percent in the 1970-80 decade and by only 1 percent from 1980 to 1985, while the national population was growing by more than 10 percent in each of those periods. However, our apparent population stability masks great flux in and out of our state.

Richard Kolhauser and Cheng H. Chiang are leading students of Illinois demography and among the first to identify the change in the mix of who we are in Illinois. They estimated that in the 1970-80 period there was a net out-migration for the white population of between 700,000 to 900,000, or up to 10 percent of all Illinois whites in 1970. From all that I can discern this net out-migration of whites has continued largely unabated in the

1980s. (Net out-migration represents the difference between the number of residents who left the state and the number who entered during the same period.)

As you might imagine, there has been a net in-migration of non-whites during the past two decades. In the 1970-80 decade there were increases of 20, 90, and more than 130 percent in Illinois populations of blacks, Hispanics, and Asians, respectively. I project that the 1990 census will show comparable continuing increases for these groups. The ratio of non-white to white population has shifted from one in thirteen in 1950 to about one in four in 1988, and the ratio will become one in three shortly after we enter the coming century.

Even if there were no more migration across our state borders, the shift would continue because of different birth rates among groups. In Chicago, for example, the average white woman has about 1.5 children in her lifetime, while the rate for blacks is 2.4 and for Hispanics 3.1 children, according to census data. Minorities now comprise 60 percent of Chicago's population, so we can describe the city with the incongruous, tongue-twisting term as "majority minority."

Minorities in Illinois comprise just 11 percent of the population among persons 65 and older, yet they make up 31 percent of the residents under 19 years of age. Between now and 1999 the white population in Illinois is projected to decrease by 3.8 percent while nonwhite residents will increase by 24 percent.

There have also been significant geographic shifts in our population. When Abraham Lincoln was contesting Stephen A. Douglas for the U.S. Senate in 1858, they focused their famed debates in central Illinois, in places like Galesburg, Ottawa, and Charleston, because 45 percent of Illinois residents were in the broad central part of the state. Today central Illinois is home to only about 15 percent of the state's populace.

Large swaths of rural Illinois have undergone longterm population decline. My home county of Stark, north of Peoria, has lost population every decade since 1880, declining from a high of 14,000 to about 6,000 in 1988. This decline has been accentuated since 1980, as a result of hard times in farming as well as in manufacturing work in nearby cities like Peoria and Moline. I sit in farm town coffeeshops and overhear folks declare they are going to hang on until "it" comes back, meaning the good ol' days, I guess. But their voices lack conviction and present a bluster that masks the fear inside.

Nor does Chicago any longer carry the population clout of its heyday. In 1920 more than half of all Illinois residents lived in Chicago; today only one in four does. On the other hand, folks are flocking to the collar counties, to work in research laboratories along the Interstate 88 corridor, and to staff service businesses that fill suburban high-rises in Schaumburg in Cook County, Naperville in DuPage County, and those farther north in Lake County. While western Illinois was losing about ten percent of its residents from just 1980 to 1988, the collar counties—often referred to as the "golden crescent"—were adding more than ten percent.

The collar counties long ago surpassed Chicago in population and now also have more residents than all of downstate's 96 counties. Not only are there more folks in the collar counties, they are younger overall. Only 7.6 percent of collar county residents are at age 65 or beyond, whereas fully 14 percent of the residents in southern Illinois are 65 and older.

The Illinois Economy

If Illinois were a nation, its 1987 gross economic product of $226 billion would make Illinois the 14th largest national economy in the world, about the same size as Spain and India and ahead of Australia, Mexico, and East Germany. Even so, the state's giant economy has been growing slowly and unevenly in recent years.

Relative to the nation, the Illinois economy has been slipping for about 40 years. In 1948 our state's average per person income was 128 percent of the national average. That figure has declined steadily, and today Illinois per capita income is about 107 percent of the national average. Our rank among the states has slipped from third highest to tenth.

Our state share of economic activity in the nation has slipped from 7.1 percent in 1950 to about 4.95 percent in 1988. These comparative figures do not mean that Illinois has been going downhill economically, just that the economies and populations of other states have been growing more rapidly.

The slow growth statewide comes from averaging the boom times in Chicago's Loop and the collar counties with conditions akin to the Depression in much of rural Illinois as well as in many urban, minority neighborhoods. Census Bureau figures for 1985 showed per capita income in DuPage County, in the heart of the collar counties, at $15,292, highest in the state. Three hundred miles to the south along the Ohio River, residents in Pulaski County generated only $6,559 per person. The highest rate of public aid recipients is not in Chicago but in Alexander County, also along the Ohio River, where 281 of every 1,000 residents are on welfare. Pulaski County has 257 per 1,000; Chicago, 212.

In 1986 I spoke to a Farm Bureau gathering in Pike County in western Illinois, once the "Pig Capital of the World." Over drinks before dinner, poker-faced farm and town leaders talked about population flight of 15 percent in the preceding decade and of unemployment of 20 percent, if everybody out of work were counted. (It is worth noting that unemployment rates do not include "discouraged workers," defined as those persons who feel there is no work to be had so have given up actively seeking work, though they would probably work if a job came along. One analyst for the state Department of Employment Security estimates the number of discouraged workers at a rate about half again the rate of reported unemployment. So if reported unemployment is 8 percent, actual joblessness could be as high as 12 percent.)

Farther up in the central region in Wyoming (population 1600), the two-story brick business building that occupies a once-prized spot on the main intersection sold a few years ago for $500; I know because it's next door to a building I own. Quite livable "starter homes" in Wyoming have been selling for as little as $4500 (you're seeing it right—no third zero)!

Extreme economic disparities exist just a few miles apart in Chicago. According to Gregory Squires and the co-authors of the 1987 book *Chicago: Race, Class, and the Response to Urban Decline*, three of the nation's 12 most affluent communities are located in Chicago. The nation's second wealthiest neighborhood is the lakefront area just north of Chicago's Loop, which boasted per capita income of $27,000 in 1984. The poorest community in the nation is located about two miles south of the Loop, in the Robert Taylor Homes public housing project where per capita income was only $1,339 in the same year. In fact, 10 of the nation's 16 most concentrated areas of poverty are located in Chicago housing projects.

We toil at different jobs in Illinois from those of the post-World War II generation. In 1947 about 40 percent of our jobs were in manufacturing; in 1988 it is only about 20 percent. On the other hand, jobs in services and finance have increased from 15 percent of the state total in 1947 to almost 30 percent in 1988. Unfortunately, the service jobs overall pay less and yet require more education than the jobs lost in manufacturing. The average annual manufacturing wage in Illinois in 1981 was $20,825 while jobs in the services sector paid an average of $14,236 the same year. Though paid less, 43 percent of Illinois men in service jobs had four years of college whereas only 15 percent of men in manufacturing had that much formal education.

Job recruiters for the new Diamond Star auto plant in Bloomington, Illinois have been going to schools in the area to say that a high school diploma alone is definitely not enough to qualify for a place on their computer- and robotics-driven workplace. Gone are the days when a young man in Peoria or Rock Island-Moline could walk away from high school without a diploma and down the street to a secure, lifetime, middle-class job "on the line" at Caterpillar or International Harvester.

What about the workforce of the future in Illinois? There will be fewer young people at work, for their numbers are way down. There were 151,000 12th graders in Illinois public high schools in 1977 but only 120,000 in 1987. This decrease in the supply of new workers presents a golden opportunity to bring down teenage unemployment, which reached 23 percent in Illinois in 1983 (50 percent among nonwhites).

How Are We Doing With Our Future Workers?

Following the November 1986 election, Governor James R. Thompson asked me to head a "transition team" that would help the thrice re-elected governor look back and then ahead, not just to the next year, but to 1999, and beyond. We held a series of retreats with agency directors, outside experts, and community leaders to find out where things stood. The mosaic we pieced together was not pretty.

The agency heads came across as real professionals, capable

and concerned, yet deeply frustrated. They were expected to do the impossible, to make an imperfect world whole, during a period of social deterioration, and to do it with inadequate, declining resources. I will not soon forget the anguished exclamation of Mike Lane, the veteran director of the Illinois Department of Corrections:

> During my years at Corrections, I've seen inmate numbers go from 5,000 to 20,000. I start receiving kids at age 13, and by that tender age they've already had an average of 10 contacts with the police.
>
> Rehabilitation? Don't ask me to do that. You know what the word means? To return to a prior state. You know the prior state of most inmates: ignorance, illiteracy, drugs, abuse! You really want me to take them back to that?

I posed the following question to the social service agency heads, including Lane. "If you had $500 million in new revenues annually, where would you put the money?" I thought that as good bureaucrats each might stake a claim on the hypothetical money. To a person they said: Put it with the littlest children, those at risk. Then maybe fewer of them will show up later in mental health institutions, on welfare, into drugs. Again, Mike Lane: "When they get to me, at 13, it's too late to do much good. Basically, we're going to have to take care of them, in our prisons, on and off throughout their lives."

In his inaugural address in 1987 Governor Thompson challenged Illinois to "adopt the Class of '99." (The members of this high school class were already four years old in 1986.) Then the Governor laid out a list of chilling social indicators to provide a profile of what the Class of '99 would look like, if things don't change.

* One of every four members of the Class of '99 will fail to graduate.

* One of every two pupils in Chicago and East St. Louis public high schools will fail to graduate.

* One in seven females in the class will become pregnant, and 8,400 of them will have at least one baby before age 18.

* The class will do about average for the nation in math; unfortunately, our nation will continue to rank dead last in math achievement among fourteen developed and developing nations against which we have been measured.

Illinois State Government

State government is only an instrument of society, and not the only one. Alone it lacks the capacity to make dramatic improvements in the outcomes of the Class of '99. Nevertheless, we do assign state government a lead role in our behalf. And we have made it a big enterprise.

If total state appropriations of about $22 billion per year were equated with business income, Illinois would rank about 12 on the Fortune 500 list of major corporations, ahead of Amoco Oil of Chicago and Procter and Gamble. The state has 120,000 employes, including those at our state universities; this is more than any Illinois-based employer other than Sears, Roebuck and Co. and McDonald's.

Illinois state government organization is about as complex as the state is diverse. By the second decade of this century, Illinois government had grown into a sprawling, unmanageable collection of more than 100 agencies, boards, and commissions. In 1917 newly-elected governor Frank O. Lowden pushed a reorganization plan through the legislature that consolidated most activities of state government into nine executive departments as set forth in a new Civil Administrative Code. Since then, the "code departments" have increased to 25; in addition there are about 50 boards and commissions linked to the governor on the organization chart because he appoints board members. When Governor James Thompson held his first cabinet meeting, in January 1977, I was present as acting director of a code department. I recall a sense of diminished importance at that "cabinet meeting" as I looked about at the 100 fellow executives and gubernatorial staff who crowded the ballroom of the Executive Mansion.

The agencies vary in size from the Department of Mental Health and Developmental Disabilities with 13,500 employes, Corrections and Public Aid with about 10,000 each, to the departments on Aging, Financial Institutions, and Nuclear Safety, with between 100 and 200 each. State government affects everyone. A few illustrations:

* The twelve social and human service agencies deliver services to 1.5 million Illinois residents each year.

* The state department for professional regulation examines, licenses, monitors, investigates, and sometimes disciplines

800,000 persons across 35 occupations, from physicians to realtors to boxers and wrestlers.
  * There are 30 million visits annually to state parks and facilities operated by the Department of Conservation.
  * Among the 20,000 inmates who crowd our 45 correctional facilities, 118 are on "death row."

As with population, state government activity has been shifting. The state capital has been moving, brick by brick, from Springfield to Chicago. Governor Thompson moved to Chicago during the second of his four terms; the Executive Mansion stands vacant. With the exception of Secretary of State Jim Edgar, our statewide elected officials and the four legislative leaders all live in Chicago and its suburbs and operate primarily from the modernistic new State of Illinois Center in the Loop. The Illinois Supreme Court now holds regular hearings in Chicago and the old State of Illinois Building in the Loop is being transformed into a state courts center. As Dave Urbanek of the suburban *Daily Herald* has written: "While Springfield is still home to the working mechanisms of state government, almost all of the major decisionmakers see Chicago's skyline when they think of state government."

Governments take in money and redistribute it, generally taking from the better off and delivering to the less well off. Illinois is no exception. Per person state government spending (for all government services and payroll) by region for 1984 shows that the five collar counties received far less back than other regions:

  * the collar counties $434
  * Cook (Chicago & all Cook) $607
  * northern region $632
  * central region $854
  * southern region $912

In addition, collar county residents overall pay more per person in state income and sales taxes than do residents of Chicago and downstate. Finally, it needs to be pointed out that collar county residents tend to tax their residential real estate at significantly higher rates than do either Chicagoans or downstaters, which suggests they may place higher value on education than do Illinoisans from other regions.

Murray Gruber of Loyola University has compiled "Yardsticks for Illinois," in which he ranks Illinois among the 50 states on a list of expenditure and "effort" indicators for education, health, and social services. As can be surmised from a look at Figure 1.1, Gruber contends that while Illinois is above average in wealth, the state is generally below average in its support of education and social welfare programs.

Liberals would probably lament this; conservatives might applaud the same data. In the chapters that follow I will argue that before we can evaluate whether these yardstick rankings for Illinois are desirable we need to:
* define a clear social contract for our purposes;
* determine the role of government therein;
* set measurable goals;
* focus on programs to accomplish the basic goals;
* determine how much it will cost and who ought to pay what,
* monitor the progress and outcomes of our work.

I hope to convince you that fundamental change in the outcomes is possible for the Class of '99 if we have the self-confidence and will to pursue these steps.

THE CHANGING FACES OF ILLINOIS 17

Figure 1.1. Yardsticks for Illinois. The ranking of Illinois among the 50 states on several educational and social service criteria.

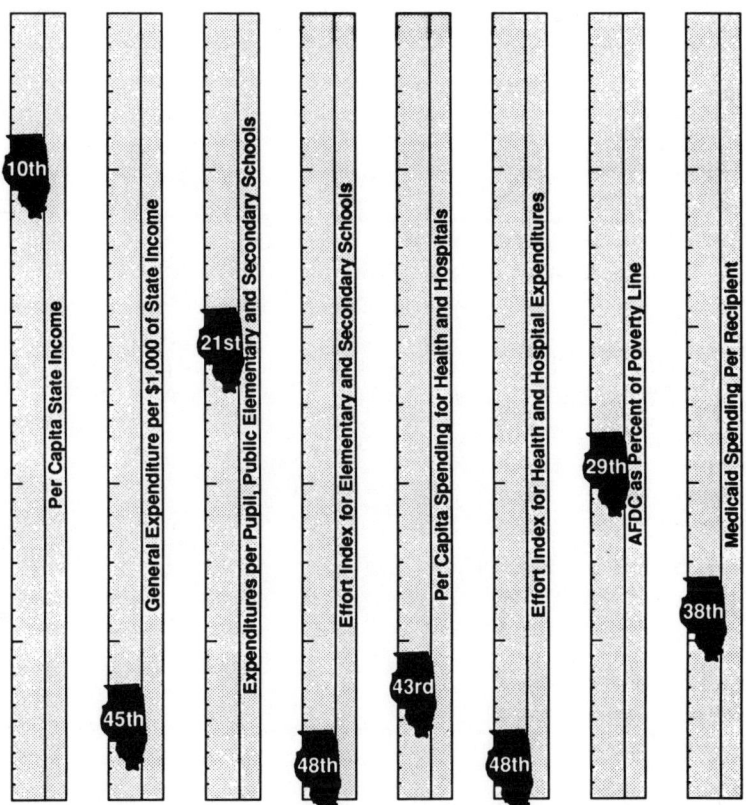

Source: Murray L. Gruber, *Yardsticks for Illinois*, Loyola University of Chicago, 1988. Effort represents state expenditures in Illinois per $1,000 of personal income as ranked among the 50 states on the same criterion.

Chapter 2

Sorting Things Out—Citizen, Community, and Government

It isn't the least government that is best, but the government that is needed least, to borrow from Illinois-based writer Jim Krohe. The larger the roles accepted by citizens and communities in fulfilling our social compact, the less we need assign to government.

Government could not do the job alone, even if we wanted it that way. As the English sociologist Richard M. Titmus put it: "You can't pay someone to love a child." Neither can government donate human organs for transplantation, nor force pregnant mothers to seek prenatal services. In talking about a 1983 crisis in Illinois foster child care (many more children than homes for them), Gordon Johnson, director of the Illinois Department of Children and Family Services (DCFS), said: "The real solution lies not with government agencies or actions. It lies with people who will open their homes and hearts to children in need."

Unfortunately, there has been erosion in our ideology of self-sufficiency and individualism. On an evening news commentary in 1987, John Chancellor pointed out that in the 1920s it was a crime in many states for Americans not to help their parents when they were able to do so. Thirty years ago, he went on, more than half of all the elderly received some help from their children, but by 1980 only four percent did. He concluded somberly that the ancient principle of helping parents is apparently no longer honored, because we expect that government will step in to help.

In my courses on public policy I ask if students have elderly members of their extended family living at home with their parents. Out of hundreds of students over recent years, only two have answered in the affirmative. Just two generations ago it was generally understood that family would take such responsibility if at all possible. Much has changed in that time. Many elderly do not want to live with their children, and they are more likely now to have the resources to live apart. There are other factors as well. Nevertheless, my students are just far enough removed that they would likely have no understanding of this transfer of responsibility for the elderly.

We have come to lean on government to relieve us of tough chores that we might have done otherwise ourselves or through community-based groups. We ask our schools to teach about sex, drugs, "excellence," and how to consume responsibly. If the local economy turns sour, we turn to government for economic development programs. Our elderly? We conclude it's irrational to help our folks out financially when the government will pay for their nursing home care. Today the federal-state Medicaid Program provides about 40 percent of all funding for nursing homes.

We enact laws to enforce citizen responsibility and then relieve the citizen of responsibility if he doesn't obey the law. 'Tis true. Illinois law requires use of auto seatbelts. In 1987, however, the Illinois Supreme Court ruled that damages to a person injured in an auto accident cannot be reduced just because the victim was not wearing a seatbelt at the time. As the *Chicago Tribune* editorialized:

> What we now have is a law that assumes people's irresponsibility. The statute requires drivers and passengers to buckle up for their own safety.... That is to say, it does not trust people to protect themselves. And now the Supreme Court says that if they fail to minimize the danger to themselves, somebody else will have to pay the cost.
>
> This is precisely backwards. It would make sense to tell drivers that seatbelts protect them financially as well as physically, since failure to wear them might reduce compensation for injury.

There is renewed interest in citizen responsibility, in the area of welfare policy at least. Liberals are joining conservatives in calling for required work, training, and education for those on public assistance. I foresee a day when this concept of reciprocity between governmental services and personal responsibility will extend, of necessity, to the middle class. For example, we realize that the cost of providing optimum health care for all citizens has outstripped available resources. We know also that certain behaviors such as smoking and high fat diets impose great health care costs on government. The U.S. Office on Smoking and Health declared in 1987 that cigarette smoking is responsible for almost 16 percent of all deaths in the United States annually.

It is easy to blame others for our behavior. In 1988 a federal court jury awarded the estate of Rose Cipollone $400,000 from a tobacco company for contributing to the lung cancer that apparently resulted from her four decades of heavy smoking. But does society through its governments have the duty to spend the same or more of its scarce resources on those who knowingly run the risk of injuring themselves than on those who discipline themselves to more prudent behavior? That is an issue few public officials will want to wrestle with, yet I predict that economic realities will force its consideration.

There are steps that can be taken now to increase citizen responsibility.

1. Heighten consciousness. A conservative center called the Freedoms Foundation has crafted a "Bill of Responsibilities." The ten articles make good sense to me. They include:

* Be fully responsible for our own actions and for the consequences of those actions.
* Respect the rights and beliefs of others...
* Give sympathy, understanding, and help to others...
* Do our best to meet our own and our families' needs...

These articles cannot be legislated. They can be reinforced in many ways. Political parties can adopt these articles, or similar ones, in their platforms. They can be proposed as guides or "tests" for legislation at the biennial conferences held to introduce newly-elected members to the state legislative process in Illinois. Newspapers can carry them regularly near their editorial page "flags."

2. Increase volunteer activity even further. There is a remarkable sense of civic responsibility among about 15-20 percent of the American citizenry. According to the Independent Sector, an organization that monitors and encourages volunteer

activity, 20 million citizens gave at least five percent of their income to the causes of their choice, and 23 million gave five or more hours per week in volunteer service. Total individual giving hit $66 billion in 1985 and the dollar value that year of all volunteer giving was estimated at more than $100 billion. The Independent Sector has a campaign going to double the numbers who "give five." If successful, the total dollar value would exceed total spending in 1985 by the U.S. departments of Health and Human Services, and Housing and Urban Development combined.

In my work on Governor Thompson's 1986 transition team I proposed that the Governor commit four or more hours per month in highly visible volunteer work, tutoring poor children at the Marillac House on Chicago's West Side for six months, then doing similar work in East St. Louis. I wrote:

> Then you could challenge everyone of us to do the same. The purpose would not be just the contribution but the increased understanding and connection among those of us in the Community of Illinois.
>
> You could take the lead in making us better than we tend to be day to day. The people up on the bluff in Fairview Heights or Belleville don't wish ill of the poor children down in the valley in East St. Louis. It's just too easy for them and us to focus on our own problems, to keep our eyes turned away.

In 1988 I served on a statewide task force on student financial aid. I proposed that we create a volunteer corps of "Lincoln Tutors" from among the 300,000-plus college students who receive significant state support to attend our public and private colleges. In return for state support that runs as high as $8,000 per student per year, the students would be asked to join in a massive program of tutoring and counseling among poor children and adolescents. The latter are the ones least likely ever to reach a point where they could also take advantage of those $8,000-per-year college aid packages.

College students already do a great deal of volunteer work. And many are so strapped already by part-time jobs that they could not become Lincoln Tutors. Nevertheless, a statewide program managed by students themselves, with the support of the Governor's Office of Volunteer Assistance, would give dramatic visibility to volunteer work. It would also link those who have made it to college with those who have not—and are not likely to without help.

3. Initiate a dialogue now on the appropriate relationships between personal responsibility/irresponsibility and public policy rewards/penalties. This could come in the format of town hall meetings at which governor and legislators seek comments from citizens on policy options for the future. By putting the matter in a future context, anxieties might be diffused a bit. Understanding could begin to develop about the tough choices that lie ahead when it comes to allocating scarce resources, in health care for example.

The Role of Community

During the "transition" mentioned earlier, DCFS director Gordon Johnson said bluntly: "The communities know a helluva lot better than we do how to deal with their people." Gubernatorial aide Jess McDonald, a former social worker, recalled that there tended to be different levels of attention paid to the young person in trouble, depending on whether "he's our problem," versus "he's the state's problem." That is, the youngster assigned to a community-based agency tended to get more personal attention than the one delivered to a state agency.

James Coleman, University of Chicago professor of education, believes that a school's success is a function of community. He contends that the more a school is seen as a part of the extended family, the better it works. Most people in need turn first to family and neighbors for help, then to their community and its churches, and then generally only as a last resort to government. In 1985, the Chapin Hall Center for Children at the University of Chicago interviewed 737 Chicagoans who headed households with children and who received public welfare. Approximately half of these families had not turned to social service providers for assistance during the year preceding the interview. "The welfare families interviewed found their help-seeking experiences with churches and private agencies to be more positive than their experiences with government social service providers."

Arthur Naperstek of the University of California confirms this:

> When low income people in ethnic subgroups are faced with

crises, the first individuals or institutions that they turn to in order of importance to them are their families, their extended family, friends, their local church, their ethnic subgroups ... institutions within their immediate environment. The eighth institution that they turn to is a professional service provider.

Robert Woodson, head of a coalition of community groups, adds: "We tend to deliver services through the institution of last choice of those in need, and we wonder why we fail."

What is it we mean by "community"? In his book about the idea of community in America, Philip Abbott identifies elements that have been central to community: a territorial base; face-to-face encounters; stability; commitment to interdependence, and shared values. Illinois is not a natural community. Our state was carved from the Northwest Territory in 1818, not around an existing community, but rather with the help of ready-made boundary lines provided by rivers and lakes. So it is understandable that in *The Nine New Nations of North America*, Henry Garreau splits Illinois into three of his proposed somewhat homogeneous "nations"—the Rust Belt, Bread Basket, and Old Dixie.

Illinois is a web of towns and small cities. The state comprises about 1,000 small towns, more than any state but Texas. Most are also communities, though often less stable and interdependent than decades ago when self-sufficiency was the *raison d'etre* of small towns and cities. Chicago is a patchwork of ethnic neighborhood communities, from that of the Irish in Bridgeport on the City's near southwest side to the Hispanic in nearby Little Village. There are scores of others, some vibrant, some breaking down.

Even self-contained space is being defined in new ways, ways that suggest the beginnings of community. There are 700 condominium units in the 100-story John Hancock Building on North Michigan Avenue in Chicago, with more residents than in my downstate hometown of Toulon (pop. 1200). The annual meeting of the "Big John" condominium association has been held in the ballroom of the Drake Hotel, up the street. It looked like a political convention, or a New England town meeting, with each floor having its own section and identifying placard. The assemblage was entertained by the John Hancock Chorus.

Woven into this colorful tapestry of communities are the nonprofit groups. There are 850,000 organizations across the nation registered with the Internal Revenue Service as "501-C-3," not-for-profit groups. In the metropolitan Chicago area there are more than 4,000 nonprofit organizations that provide direct services to people, with total expenditures in 1984 of $8.4 billion, the equivalent of nine percent of the region's personal income.

Hospitals and educational institutions generate the lion's share of activity among these Chicago-area groups. In addition to these two sectors there are 3,000 other human service agencies, with budgets totalling $2.5 billion, bigger in 1984 than the Chicago corporate budget of $1.9 million. Most of these nongovernmental agencies are small, and half were created since 1970. They derive their budgets roughly one-third each from governments, earned income, and charitable contributions.

Illinois state government could not function without these nonprofit groups nor without its local governments. There are 6,500 local government units in Illinois, more than in any other state. Two of every three dollars from our state general revenue fund go to the local level, in distributions to community schools and in grants to nonprofit social service providers. For example, the Jewish Federation of Chicago is playing a lead role for the Illinois Department of Public Aid in the administration of its refugee assistance program. Chicago area black churches and the state children services agency (DCFS) have teamed up for the "One Church, One Child" adoption program. DCFS contracts child care services through 230 local groups and agencies. Four private agencies in the Peoria area proposed in 1987 to DCFS that they assume complete responsibility for all foster care in the Peoria region.

The interdependency is so tight that it is hard to tell what is government, nonprofit, and for profit. As illustration, more than 90 percent of the budget of Catholic Charities of Illinois, a sprawling network of social service agencies, comes from governments. (So much for separation of church and state, not that I fault this working relationship, so long as services are delivered well and efficiently.) The University of Illinois is a $1 billion a year public institution that generates 60 percent of its income from outside the state General Revenue Fund. It operates a major hospital in Chicago that provides services paid for largely by other government agencies, principally the Department of Public Aid. The U. of I. has considered contracting all hospital management out to a for-profit company.

During the 1986-87 transition, we wrestled with the idea of empowering communities further in efforts to address pressing problems. The following is taken from a memorandum I provided Governor Thompson as background for his fourth inaugural address:

> Basically, we at the State level do too much telling, and not enough listening. We deliver services for narrow purposes through narrowly focused agencies, for income support, for food stamps, for mental health, public health, rehabilitation.
>
> We need more flexibility and coordination across agencies at the state level, and, at the local level, more integration of services and greater involvement of community leadership.
>
> And here I emphasize that a focus on local community is not a way out of our state responsibility. No, it is the road to our responsibility.
>
> Nor do I believe that those in communities are inherently more virtuous that those of us in state government. Both comprise good people, and flawed people. Yet those in the communities and neighborhoods are closer to, more savvy about, and more concerned about their own, than are persons more distant.

The Governor did develop the theme of "taking government services back home, to our communities and neighborhoods." Staff work churned for awhile as a result. Below are excerpts from a February 1987 memo by Jess McDonald to Deputy Governor Jim Reilly:

> The responsibility for responding to human services problems has been increasingly fixed on state government. The federal government has sought to limit its role and its financial commitment by encouraging states to assume the responsibility for these services. Local governments have played a limited role, with some exceptions, in human services, looking instead to state government to resolve the problems of kids, the mentally ill, etc.
>
> Some communities have established a commitment to serve and have taxed themselves in order to maintain their involvement. Others participate through strong voluntary efforts such as the United Way, the various charities and non-profit organizations in general. This is evidenced especially in child welfare services but also in a full range of human needs.

Community-based organizations have consistently supported state human service agencies but have contended that even with the same resources they could more effectively serve the same people the state serves. No other issue in child welfare sparks as much debate as this one.

In fact, state agencies deliver most services through voluntary and other community based agencies. Even while we purchase most services, we do not usually grant extensive flexibility to community agencies to respond to needs we the state identify. We speak of the strength, will and creativity of the community but we do not encourage or welcome the community's critique of our performance or its suggestions for change.

For instance, four private agencies in Peoria, including Catholic Charities, proposed assuming responsibility for all DCFS foster care in the Peoria region. They have not even received an evaluation of the proposal or a formal response. The proposal is a radical suggestion in some respects but perhaps it has strong merit. It seems we should encourage, not discourage, such thinking and proposals. If the proposals have merit we should be flexible enough to explore implementation and implement if it makes sense. The Community Innovations Initiative would do that exactly.

The Governor could solicit proposals in much the same way that the White House has invited states to submit ideas for welfare reform demonstration projects. It is essentially an invitation, a challenge and an opportunity. We would pledge our support of worthy and affordable projects and agree to cut red tape and make the bureaucracy responsive.

Some agencies will cringe at the thought of opening up for challenge and change the current methods of operations. Others will put opportunities on the table. The Department of Mental Health and Developmental Disabilities, for instance, would use this as an opportunity to explore Mental Health Task Force implementation options. The Department of Public Aid might find some communities willing to carve out a role in welfare reform.

The strength of the transition effort was that it forced us to think and re-think how we do business. The "Community Concept" that was advanced by the transition effort has promise but needs form and structure. We have an opportunity to challenge further the way we choose to respond to human needs. It need not be more of the same.

There are shortcomings and pitfalls in this concept of increased decentralization of activity to the local, community level. It is a truism that each community is unique. Some are rich in human resources, have effective functioning groups and strong leadership capacity. Others are nearly depleted on all counts. Thus community responsiveness is going to vary greatly. David Menefee-Libey is a researcher at the Rand Center in Washington, D.C. He has observed and worked with local community groups in Chicago. He cautions that community organizations in poor neighborhoods tend to be valuable as advocates but are often much less effective as program administrators. He has found that they tend to resist the responsibility for allocating scarce program resources among their neighbors.

Second, you cannot decentralize services provided by state government without first involving the communities. In the 1970s Illinois and many states embarked on a grand experiment in "deinstitutionalization" of our state mental health institutions. We nearly emptied our "schools" for the retarded and our "hospitals" for the mentally ill, on the premise that these unfortunate citizens would get better, more caring attention in their own community facilities, and that this approach would cost less.

Unfortunately, we basically forgot to tell the communities what was afoot, nor did we transfer funds adequate to meet the communities' new responsibilities. The concept made sense; the implementation was miserable. The increased numbers of mentally-ill homeless on our streets is one result.

I believe that we can take more of government back home to our communities. The lessons we learned the hard way in mental health can be instructive in forging stronger partnerships back home. In years to come I see the potential for a "comprehensive community aid formula," along the lines of our long-standing school aid formula, in which state resources are distributed to reward local effort and to compensate for lack of local wealth.

Fundamental Government

Government is a powerful tool of organized society. In the past 20 years governments in the U.S. have nearly abolished hunger, improved air and water quality, and increased overall prosperity among the elderly. On the other hand, governments have not ended poverty and may even have increased the dependence of the underclass on government, the opposite of the desired outcome.

The question becomes then: What do we want government to try to do and not do? Eighteenth Century philosopher John Locke thought the sole mission of the state was to provide protection and security. Rousseau would have assigned a somewhat more expansive role to government, for he felt the state was essential to an environment conducive to the intellectual and moral development of man.

Until this century, governmental services had been quite basic. The Northwest Ordinance of 1787 set aside the 16th section of each 36-section congressional township for the support of education, and the countryside blossomed with little red or white one-room schoolhouses. The Morrill Land Grant Act of 1862 provided resources to develop our unprecedented system of public universities, a network unmatched in the world.

Local governments stepped in to care for the homeless. As a youngster, I remember riding my bicycle several miles south of town—Mother never knew I roamed quite that far—on the blacktop past the "ol' county poor farm." I was fascinated by the cemetery where tiny, rough grave markers denoted the names of those who ended their days at "the farm." Old-timers have told me life was so basic there that folks worked hard to avoid the fate of ending up at the farm. Nevertheless, it appears local governments may have done better then than now in caring for the homeless.

Government services were added when communities felt a need to organize publicly to fulfill a social compact responsibility that community could not handle informally. We had community hospitals, community fire protection districts, and community libraries, the last often with the help of "robber baron" and philanthropist Andrew Carnegie. I even played on Saturday nights on the courthouse square with the Toulon Municipal Band, for which a band tax of one or two cents per hundred dollars of property valuation was levied.

Since the Depression of the 1930s, government has become more intertwined in our lives. The *Wall Street Journal* pointed out several years ago that slightly more than half of all Americans who receive income receive all or a major portion of their income from one or another government, or from a government-oriented industry such as the defense industry. This includes government workers at all levels; public school teachers; social security and welfare recipients, and military retirees, among others. About 80 percent of the national government domestic budget—more than $450 billion—is devoted to cash or in-kind transfers to individuals.

Once in place, Big Government seeks reasons to expand. The following comment by an observer in London's *Sunday Times* generated a chuckle from me, because of the writer's evident exasperation with the growth of local government since World War II in the United Kingdom. It is apt for us as well:

> Activity is contagious and if an institution is stirred up and made to do certain things it will soon, of its own volition, find other important tasks to which it must turn its hand. Thus we have arrived at the present, where essential local services include making the borough a nuclear-free zone, twinning it with Timbuktu and ensuring that the children in its schools understand the nature and practices of homosexuality.

My friend Bill Campbell the journalist, whose cartoons you see in this book, says his fraternity has contributed to our growing focus on government as our problem solver:

> When I was covering local affairs for the Galesburg (IL) *Register-Mail*, we never thought to report regularly on the social service activities of the council of churches or the YMCA, but when the feds—through LBJ's Great Society—set up local community action agencies, we added them to our beat automatically, because they were "public," even though the nonprofits were undoubtedly providing more social services.

Over recent decades policymakers have constructed ungainly, jerrybuilt governmental structures. While each element probably made sense when added, the sum is less than the total of its parts. In the late 1970s I co-chaired a state task force to look at school requirements, or mandates. We found 16 instructional mandates the state had imposed on local schools. These included consumer education, physical ed, driver's ed, career ed, conservation ed, family life, patriotism, birds and trees, the state constitution, drugs and alcohol abuse, and safe bus-riding practices. As a result, there is precious little time left for the core curriculum of languages, literature, math, and science. Yet try to remove a mandate and a teachers' union or parent group rises up in arms.

What is it we want? Public opinion polls show that people want less government, want government "to get off our backs," yet oppose cutting any program that benefits them. There is also confusion. Because our national, state, regional, and local governments do so much, we do not understand all they do, nor how they could be spending so much of our money. As a consequence, there is growing concern over getting one's "fair share." Governments take in about one-third of our gross national product, and redistribute much of it back to individuals and communities, so there is understandable interest in getting "our fair share" back.

I have heard social service executives refer to this as the "Du Page problem." Du Page County is the largest of the counties in the collar around Cook County, with three-quarters of a million residents. This county of generally middle- and upper-middle class whites is thought by many social service providers to be politically resistant to policies for poor blacks that would take more tax money from Du Page and return nothing. For example, in 1987 the public schools in East St. Louis (pop. 50,000) received $48 million in state school aid, while the schools in all of Du Page County, with 15 times as many residents, received only $45 million.

This concern over a fair share is often heard downstate as well, where residents think they are drained of taxes at the expense of Chicago. Overall, they are wrong. As noted in Chapter 1, per capita state funding for all state government services in 1984 showed that the collar counties, including Du Page, were big "losers" while downstate and Chicago were "winners."

Governments serving large populations have always redistributed wealth. Poor kids in the ghettos simply need more financial support than do those in fashionable Oak Brook in Du Page County. Underlying the "fair share" concerns, however, is a sense of futility among taxpayers in better off communities. I've heard often: "I'd pay more if I thought it would make a difference, but dammit, I don't think it will." The *Chicago Tribune*, a crusader for greater attention to the plight of the urban underclass, has found the same sentiment:

32   A NEW GAME PLAN FOR ILLINOIS

Yet there is a growing acceptance of the underclass as an unfortunate but unavoidable offshoot of modern urban life. Some traditional liberals as well as conservatives are saying, "We've tried everything and nothing worked. Seal them off as best we can and concentrate on helping the deserving poor."

We lack a compass in Illinois to give us a heading to our future, and we lack clear, credible, measurable approaches that might give taxpayers more confidence that we can make a significant difference with their hard-earned tax dollars. Candidates tend to promise to do more and better with less. Joe and Mary Citizen are understandably preoccupied with family and careers, and provide little guidance. Most citizens are now represented by one or more interest groups that protect existing programs, but which have no organizational reason to take an interest in broader public issues.

How then can we clarify our purposes and fundamental responsibilities to one another? In the chapter that follows I propose that we rethink our social contract, focus on the next generation, and set specific measurable goals.

Chapter 3

Goals for Illinois

I spent the summer of 1987 in Geneva, Switzerland where I reviewed the development of social contract theory. I worked in the reading room at the University of Geneva, situated directly above a museum devoted to a native son, Jean-Jacques Rousseau, author of *Le Contrat Social*.

One morning I returned to the library from the local train station, where American friends, based in Switzerland with multinational companies, were seeing their children off for a week of Boy Scout camping in the Alps. Single, I am not around children much. So I was struck by the great helpings of love, guidance and encouragement that the assembled parents heaped on their young charges. I am sure it is much the same in Chicago's suburbs and other comfortable places.

Not so in East St. Louis, the last place I was around children, a summer earlier. That depleted city of 50,000 blacks is hell's half acre. In October 1988 many more East St. Louis residents were on state welfare rolls (22,000) than were employed (13,000). Most of the children reside with one parent, often a semi-literate child-mother. At best, one in five of the eligible children receives Head Start-type help. Pimps and pushers are the likely role models. Few are off to camp. Hope? What hope?

In Geneva I began to wonder if Rousseau had children in mind when he drafted his version of a social contract. Probably not, though he did speak of *pitié* (compassion) along with selfishness, as parts of human nature. And he did write of government as the servant of the general will of the people.

At that time, however, contract theory emphasized limiting the state, not extending it. Yet relationships among citizens and their governments evolve, as from our own Pilgrims' Mayflower

Compact to the proposed Port Huron Statement of student activists of the 1960s. Our compact in Illinois has come to embrace general state support for just about everything, from county fairs to fisheries to the arts to a new stadium for the White Sox.

What about for the dependent, vulnerable children of East St. Louis? Give a pop opinion survey and I am confident most Americans would agree that all children ought to have comparable opportunities to develop their learning skills. Yet the opportunity gap between have and have-not children appears to be widening. Why?

Several factors contribute. Many Americans have developed a sense of futility that anything will work, that we are "losing ground" in spite of huge government expenditures. We know now, however, that some things do work. The Perry Preschool Project in Michigan documented the positive change in young adults from poor backgrounds, as a result of intensive, very early childhood programs. Philanthropist Eugene Lang has made a dramatic difference in the graduation rates for his adopted pupils in East Harlem in New York City.

GOALS FOR ILLINOIS   35

Second, over the years we have added programs to the government agenda that try to do just about everything, solve every problem. As a result, our jerrybuilt compact is overloaded with marginal programs, so much so that fundamental purposes suffer. The school mandates cited in the preceding chapter provide a good illustration.

We need to sort things out in our compact with one another.

There is urgency—as well as opportunity—to this matter of social compact. As noted in the preceding chapter, the number of young people entering our job market has been declining, and will continue to do so. There are expected to be more than enough jobs for those prepared to handle them. But if our school math scores continue to rank at the bottom among the 14 nations with which the U.S. was recently compared, and if half our inner-city public high school students continue to drop out before graduation, then good jobs will go begging.

In *Tales of a New America*, Robert Reich holds that "the most important function of a political culture is not the crafting or evaluation of new solutions but rather the act of defining core problems." I suggest that before we get to those definitions we need to understand as clearly as possible what we as a society want to achieve, and how we ought to assign responsibilities and obligations among citizens, communities, and governments.

Over the centuries, social contracts have represented statements of existing or desired affairs. Running through all social contracts, explicit or implicit, has been the understanding that the rights and duties of the state and its citizens are reciprocal, that is, both the state *and* citizens have responsibilities. I sense that today we tend to think only in terms of governments' responsibilities to us.

Pericles and J. S. Mill are among those who have reminded us across history that states ought to be evaluated in terms of 1) the types of persons and character they produce among citizens and 2) the opportunities they offer all citizens to develop. In *Statecraft as Soulcraft* present-day observer George Will notes that in a liberal democratic society the state also needs give ample scope to the motives of personal ambition and accumulation. He adds, rather quickly, that the political system must incorporate unselfish motives as well, in the interests of its own stability if for no better reasons. "Altruism—principled regard for others—is not optional," Will says. "It is necessary for strengthening the sense of community that the theory and practice of modern politics attenuates."

Will says this altruism is associated in contemporary domestic policies with the phrase the "welfare state," that these are the policies that express the community's acceptance of an "ethic of common provision." In *Statecraft as Soulcraft* he notes that conservatives are fond of the metaphor of a footrace; that is:

> All citizens should be roughly equal at the starting line of the race of life. But ... (knowledge about) early childhood development suggests that "equality of opportunity" is a much more complicated matter than conservatives can comfortably acknowledge. Prenatal care . . ., infant stimulation, childhood nutrition and especially home environment—all these and other influences affect the competence of a young "runner" as he or she approaches the academic hurdles that so heavily influence social outcomes in America . . .

Not only is this idea of getting children to the same starting line for the footrace of life one that conservatives embrace; it also represents the dominant ideology in the United States, that of an individualism in which society offers individuals an equal starting point in the meritorious competition for economic success.

The problem is that we have such a strong psychological need to believe in the "equal starting line" ideology that we will accept the illusion of it when the reality would shame us. For example, education reforms that sprouted in most states in the early 1980s have already begun to wilt, markedly so in Illinois as will be documented later, and disillusionment is spreading. *Chicago Tribune* columnist Joan Beck summarizes the situation: 1) the number of kids with high risk of failure grows; 2) the percentage of children for whom English is not the primary language increases; 3) legislatures, including Illinois, have come up woefully short in promised funding for reform initiatives.

Children on the valley floor in East St. Louis do not arrive at the same starting point for formal education as do those up on the bluff. Most will never catch up.

Focus on the Next Generation

Where are we going? We don't seem to know. It has been this way before. In his memoirs of the 1930s, William Shirer (noted also for chronicling the rise and fall of the Third Reich) writes of the U.S. in 1939: "Where are we Americans going? No one knew. We were racing hell-bent to somewhere. That, to most people, seemed enough." World War II came along and gave us a cause, a mission we're lacking today.

I propose a mission that ought to be compelling to Illinois residents—our children. A decade ago the aged comprised the poorest segment in our society; now it is our children. A child under six today is six times more likely to be poor than a person over 65. Almost one of every four children in Illinois under the age of six grows up in poverty, often with one parent who is herself likely to be an ill-educated teenager. The footrace of life begins here with these littlest children and their child-mothers.

About half of one's intellectual capacity is developed by the time a child is four and 80 percent by age eight, according to Benjamin Bloom of the University of Chicago. As another specialist says: "The first five years are the most important of your life. That's when you get your first idea of what the world is, whether it's a safe place to be . . . . Is it going to be cold and hostile, painful and hungry? Or is somebody going to come and take care of you?" For too many of the children in East St. Louis and places like it the world is a scary, dark place where they develop bitter, hateful attitudes that are difficult to shake.

Facility with language is central to success later in life. A survey by kindergarten teachers in Chicago public schools found that barely half their kindergarten pupils could say both their names and few could name any of the primary colors. The same survey was administered by kindergarten teachers in Wilmette, an upper-middle class suburb north of Chicago; as you might have expected, most Wilmette children were able to recite these basics. Economist Lester Thurow says that we need not worry so much about youngsters from communities like Wilmette; they will generally become quite productive citizens. He says the problem is that the bottom half of Japan's workforce is beating the pants off our bottom half.

We know that early childhood education programs work. The report *Changed Lives* follows children from the Perry

Preschool Program in Ypsilanti, Michigan to age 19; the program was begun in 1962. These children from poor economic backgrounds had higher grade-point averages through their school years than did similar kids from a control group who did not receive the special help. In addition, they spent fewer years in special education classes, had higher graduation rates (67 percent versus 49 percent), more continued their education after high school (38 percent compared with 21 percent), and had higher rates of employment and earnings. And fewer of the females experienced early pregnancies.

The Chicago school board has traced 577 pupils from their early child-and-parent centers (for ages 3 and 4) up through third grade. These children had average grade level reading scores of 3.6, while other low income children in the system scored 3.0 (the national average was 3.8).

I have observed children in day care centers on Chicago's devastated West Side at the Marillac House and the Ogden-Millard Center. The kids are vibrant, alert, positive, and inquisitive. This is remarkable when one looks outside the windows to the bleak settings that envelop the children. Psychologist Ken Magid says, "If we attended to the early bonding crisis (between child and loved ones) in America and to our children's well being, we could eliminate half of all senseless psychopathic crime within two generations."

The sad fact is that we are simply creaming from our poorest children. We take the one in five we think might make it, and focus our thin resources with him or her, abandoning the rest to their almost hopeless childhood battlegrounds. Head Start for little kids works, yet only one in five eligible receives this jump start to a better life. Early childhood programs in Illinois, ballyhooed with "education reforms" of 1985, reach an even smaller fraction.

Goals for Illinois

Rarely do we read about measurable goals in a political party platform or hear a candidate or public official set specific objectives. Instead, we hear vague promises to do "more" and "better," to improve education and reduce crime. Can you remember a candidate for governor ever setting measurable goals for high school graduation rates and reductions in teen pregnancies? Are we afraid to be held accountable? Do we lack confidence that we can achieve significant change? Are there too many variables at work beyond the control of public officials?

But times are changing. In return for voter support for a big property tax boost, Evanston school administrators and teachers bound themselves to goals in which students with five years' tenure in the school system would perform overall at the 85th percentile of students nationally, with at least 80 percent of all students performing at the 50th percentile. A civic group working for Chicago school reform has proposed goals wherein 50 percent of all students would be above national averages within five years, and that dropout rates would be reduced five percent each of those five years. There is no magic in goals, yet they can tell much about us—about our aspirations, our compact with one another, our confidence and commitment. In addition, goals can be important tools to focus our attention and to hold us accountable.

Throughout 1987-88 Governor James Thompson worked unsuccessfully for an increase in the income tax, to go primarily for education and social services. During this time I conducted an unscientific survey on the issue, in coffeeshops and on the street. Most folks wanted to see improvements in education, but they tended to oppose the tax increase, basically because they did not think more money would make any difference in the outcomes. That is the problem. We lack confidence in the political system to make a difference. In response to this dilemma, I wrote an opinion essay for the *Chicago Tribune* that was directed to state lawmakers:

Get tough, I said. Bargain tough, just as the Illinois Education Association bargains tough with school boards. Negotiate contracts with government agencies that have specific, measurable goals. Make them four- year contracts, as a single year or even a biennium is not long enough to assess change. Most of you will be around in four years to evaluate compliance, and to impose rewards or sanctions. Here are illustrations of quadrennial goals and requirements you might set, in return for more money from a tax increase.

To the state school board: Contract with us to increase Illinois high school graduation rates by five percentage points, from 75 to 80 percent, and to improve the average ACT test scores by two points, from 19 to 21. Increase statewide high school math achievement levels from about 60 percent to 80 percent of those achieved in Japan.

To the Chicago school board: Increase average ACT scores in Chicago public high schools from 11.9 to 15 and reduce dropout rates five percent each year. To each social service agency: Sit down with our legislative staff and set two performance goals to be achieved within four years. (The state budget book includes performance indicators, yet overall they are not taken seriously.)

The agencies will likely resist these or any goals, saying there are too many unforeseen variables. If so, tell the agency: "Okay, then lay out some goals you can meet. If you cannot give us any, does that confirm our fears that more taxes won't buy us more or better services?"

Be tough. No goals, no new taxes. They will come around, for you have policy options that carry real clout. With the public schools it's the voucher concept. As for the social service agencies, you can reorganize them with a vengeance, or dismantle them in large part and contract directly with community-based organizations.

Take the contract home to "your members," that is, constituents, to see if they like the terms. Once you sign your contracts, nail them to the wall in the Capitol rotunda, where the United Way thermometer goes now, so the terms and goals are not forgotten. That is the type of bargaining for which this taxpayer would pay extra, I said in conclusion.

Are these goals achievable, unreasonable, too modest? Worth pursuing? Less important than others? Our answers would tell us much about ourselves. I believe each *is* achievable, though the challenge in East St. Louis and similar depleted neighborhoods is most daunting. We must pursue goals like these if we are to compete in the next century. Now we need a plan to achieve the goals.

Chapter 4

Productivity and Education

The premise underlying public concern about education reform is that productivity and wealth are largely functions of education quality. A quarter century ago the Japanese Economic Council stated: "Economic competition is technical competition, and technical competition has become educational competition." Xerox chairman David Kearns says simply: "Education is a bigger factor in productivity growth than increased capital, economics of scale or better allocation of resources." It is as if teachers, professors, and supportive parents are becoming the machine tools of the post-industrial age, in which information and information processing are the raw material and the machinery of a new economic order.

In *Who Gets Ahead*, Christopher Jencks of Harvard reports that when an individual first enters the labor market, the highest grade of schooling achieved is the best single predictor of one's eventual occupational status. It explains about half the variance in a person's work status. Education achievement is also the strongest predictor of income, and income differences by education attainment appear to be widening. Figure 1 shows real family income to be dropping for those with less than college preparation, while growing significantly for families headed by college graduates.

Measuring against ourselves, the U.S. has done remarkably well in elevating the percentages of us who are graduated from high school and college. According to the Census Bureau, among people 25-29 in 1940, only five percent were college graduates and 40 percent held high school diplomas. By 1984 for the same age group, 22 percent were college grads and 86 percent had at least high school diplomas or high school equivalency certificates.

Table 4.1 Median family income by educational attainment of head in constant 1985 dollars.

Educational Attainment	1975	1980	1985	Change 80-85
Less Than 8 Years	$14,854	$14,157	$13,549	- 4.3%
8 Years Elementary	21,245	18,441	17,793	- 3.5
1 to 3 Years High School	22,902	21,168	19,213	- 9.2
4 Years High School	29,458	28,539	27,472	- 3.7
1 to 3 Years College	33,158	32,486	32,177	- 1.0
4 Years College	41,276	40,314	43,187	+ 7.1
5 Years or More College	46,340	45,386	50,525	+11.3

Source: Current Population Reports, Series P-60, Bureau of the Census, U.S. Department of Commerce.

Unfortunately, we can no longer be content to measure solely against ourselves. Other nations are outstripping us. Here are some comparative figures for the U.S. and Japan, provided by the national education departments of the two nations:

	U.S.	Japan
literacy rate	80%	99%
high school graduation rate	73%	94%
length of school year	180 days	240 days
teacher salaries compared to other wage earners	approx. average for all workers	in top 10% of all wage earners

It is true that about half of U.S. high school grads go on to take some college work, a much higher percentage than in Japan. The Japanese more than compensate for this by providing intensive training programs within their industries and businesses. Their people are prepared for their jobs at whatever level of skill required. Alarming numbers of Americans are not. Thomas Espenshade of the Urban Institute estimates that a decade from now three quarters of all new jobs will require some college or special skills while only half of all new workers are likely to have gone beyond high school.

In 1987 the New York Telephone Company gave a simple 50-

minute exam in basic reading and reasoning skills to 21,000 applicants for entry-level jobs. Only 16 percent passed. It was not a problem for the company, as they had many more applicants than job openings. That luxury will soon be a thing of the past, however, as jobs are growing much faster than is the number of new workers. That same year Chicago businesses made 4,000 summer jobs available for youth. Two thousand five hundred jobs went unfilled because applicants could not handle the simple writing and figuring skills required, even though many applicants were graduates of Chicago public high schools.

As a result, American businesses are investing heavily in the most basic training and education. Sixteen corporations established a Corporate/Community School in Chicago in 1988. There were 2,000 applicants for the 150 openings in this school located in the poor, black North Lawndale neighborhood. Children will enroll at age 2, and the school will be open from 7 in the morning until 7 in the evening; there will be day care and "latch key" services before and after regular school hours. But American business has enough challenges of its own. It cannot also shoulder the fundamental task of education. That resides with parents, communities, and government.

Real Education Reform

As I drafted this section on New Year's Day 1988, the Sunday *New York Times* of the same date devoted four major stories to the topic of education reform. My education file drawer bulges with news clips and reports calling for change. Illinois focused on the issue in 1985, a couple of years later than many states; 240 proposals for change were presented to the Illinois General Assembly that year. "Sweeping reforms" were adopted, or so trumpeted the legislature's press releases.

The lawmakers approved major reading improvement grants, pilot programs for 3-4 year olds at risk of failure, state reimbursement for full day kindergarten in all schools, and school report cards to inform the public about their school's performance compared with other schools. These were important steps, but there was no talk of fundamental change, as in longer school days and more of them. Even with increased funding that year, state per pupil support was still 14 percent

44 A NEW GAME PLAN FOR ILLINOIS

below that of 1977, adjusted for inflation, according to the Chicago Panel on Public School Finances, an education watchdog group.

What has taken place between 1985 and 1988? Not much. A math and science academy for gifted children has been established. Several pilot programs have been initiated for drop-out prevention and at-risk kids. But the number of at-risk preschool children served has decreased from 16,500 out of 112,000 eligible to about 6,900 served in 1988 and 11,000 for 1989. Basically the reforms are not being funded.

There have even been steps backward. The powerful teacher unions were successful in enacting legislation that extends the seniority criterion for personnel decisions from certified personnel (teachers) to noncertified employes. As a result, school district boards and administrators have less authority than ever to manage their operations.

Illinois adopted "painless reform;" that is, it looks good on paper, avoids the pain of a tax increase to fund it, and avoids stepping on the toes of the teacher unions. Real reform is not without pain. The Spanish-speaking have a saying, *"Vale la pena"* (it is worth the pain or effort). Here are proposals for change that will cost money and step on toes. I believe they would *vale la pena*.

1. Focus on outcomes rather than process.
2. Provide school districts and administrators real authority and responsibility for their outcomes.
3. Institute longer school days and school years.
4. Provide intensive early childhood programs for every child at risk.
5. Recruit good teachers with the promise of good pay *and* professional respect.
6. Give schools that perform poorly the right to fail.

Rather than go into detail about each proposal, which would extend this book to a length akin to *War and Peace*, let me explain briefly those that are not self-explanatory. For example, education officials and state lawmakers have traditionally been intrigued by the school processes that lead to outcomes, rather than with the actual outcomes, or performance.

The state "School Code" of education statutes is about an

inch thick. It comprises more than 220 specific mandates that tell what must be taught and in what ways. Case in point: The state mandates that public schools offer driver training. Fine. But why mandate exactly "30 clock-hours of classroom instruction and 6 clock-hours of behind the wheel instruction" over a long list of topics that must be covered, including that of the "Litter Control Act" as it pertains to auto use. Many students might well be able to learn to drive safely in fewer classroom hours. They could use the time saved on core courses like languages, math, and science, which are being squeezed mercilessly by similar instructional mandates.

The statutes tell also who is qualified to be hired and who may be dismissed. School boards, superintendents, and principals have little authority in such fundamental matters. In a compelling article in the Spring 1988 *Public Interest*, John Chubb reports that his research on school performance persuades him that the key is the local school institution, its leadership and teamwork among administrators and teachers. For him, autonomy is critical, not the rigid state control we have institutionalized in state statutes.

Our school calender was adopted to meet the workforce needs of an agrarian society. Our students are simply going to have to work longer and harder. Maybe not 6-day weeks, 240 days a year as in Japan, but at least the 210 days a year as in West Germany, in place of 176 days in Illinois. And longer each day—the Japanese attend school 7 hours a day versus 5 1/2 or 6 hours a day here. And harder—65 percent of Japanese high schoolers spend five or more hours per week on homework versus 24 percent of students in the U.S. I am not an expert on this matter, and I do not think we ought to copy the Japanese in every detail, yet common sense compels me to the conclusion that one can learn more in 240 days than in 176, *if* well-taught by stimulating teachers in both cases.

We must also provide more support for many poor children in the 60 months from birth until they enter formal schooling. Black newspaper columnist William Raspberry quotes at length from an educator friend of his. It is worth repeating:

> Why do so many of the kids of the very poor seem dumber than the kids of the middle- and upper-income families? Several things may be operating to "dumb them down."

One is poor parenting by stressed and ignorant and often single young people, even adolescents—parenting that not only fails to stimulate the babies and toddlers and children, but which actually stifles their natural curiosity...

A youngster who grows up in that bleak environment is going to be no intellectual match for kids who grow up in stimulating, encouraging households filled with good talk, books, and reinforcement for all the stages of child development.

In addition, some of these kids in poverty are in lead-laden environments where, after a few years, they are not just "dumbed down," they are brain-damaged as well. Plus, they are apt to have poor diets. The good eater will beat out the poor eater every time.

The educator says the logical approach is to "address the range of problems which are, after all, not mysteries, but already well known—problems with solutions, starting with prenatal care and running through parenting skills, good nutrition, clean environments, early childhood 'educare' or Head Start experiences, and then into schools staffed by teachers who care and are well trained to provide that mixture of nurture and teaching that all youngsters require."

We know what to do and how to do it. But we are not doing it.

The above paragraphs make clear that the classroom alone can never become sufficient to generate the most from our youngsters. Encouragement, support, discipline will also be needed, from family, teachers, role models. That said, the classroom and teachers are becoming ever more important in the lives of children, because children are spending less and less time with parents. This results from the increases in single-parent families and in working mothers. Children probably spend more waking hours with teachers than with parents.

What kinds of role models do the teachers provide? What expectations, ambitions, aspirations, and goals do the teachers have for themselves and their young charges? Aimes McGuiness, associate director of the Education Commission of the States, points out that in recent decades most teachers have come from the bottom quartile of our college student bodies in terms of scores on achievement tests. He worries that teachers from this lowest stratum of achievement may have lower expectations for themselves and for their pupils than would college students who are from the top half or top quarter of college ranks.

If so it becomes critical that we recruit more teachers of the future from among our best and brightest. How do we do that? We pay them well, as in Japan, and we treat them with respect by making them a part of the decision-making process in the local schools. This will be expensive and it will require better administrators as well.

Finally, since I have proposed giving local schools authority to go with the responsibility they have always had, we would be able to hold them accountable for their performance. If they fail, they should fold. Businesses can fail, and do all the time; close to 800,000 went under in the U.S. in 1987. The threat of failure provides quite an incentive not to fail, not to lose everything, including self-esteem. Governments are apparently not capable of failing, for they rarely go out of business.

New Jersey governor Thomas H. Kean believes local school districts ought to have the right to fail. He signed legislation several years ago that gives the state power to remove the superintendent and school board if a school district fails to correct serious problems over the course of a multi-year monitoring process. They would be replaced by state agents or by a neighboring school district. In 1988 he called the bluff of the 30,000-pupil Jersey City school district. They are still wrangling in court over the state's right to take over schools, but ultimately the state will prevail, as schools and local governments are creatures of the state.

There is one district in Illinois that neither the state nor any neighboring school district could take over, even though it has clearly failed. It is the Chicago public school system.

The Albatross Around Illinois' Neck

The Chicago public school system is the third largest in the U.S., with 400,000 pupils in 600 school buildings. Three in five of the pupils are black; 24 percent are Hispanic; 13 percent are white. Nearly half the pupils live in poverty, the majority of this half without fathers at home. Former Secretary of Education William Bennett repeatedly pinned the label of "worst in the nation" on the Chicago school system, for all the world to see.

Thirty-five of the 65 Chicago public high schools rank in the *bottom one percent* of all U.S. high schools in terms of achievement test scores! Fewer than half who enter high school are graduated; in several schools only ten percent make it to graduation. In 1984 the system graduated only 9,500 black and Hispanic young people out of 25,000 originally enrolled as ninth graders. Only 2,000 of those who did graduate could read at or above the 12th grade level. The average American College Testing score for Chicago public high schoolers in 1986 was 11.9 out of a possible 36. For students in Chicago area suburban public high schools the average was 19.8. (For a graphic view from inside the system see the *Chicago Tribune's* May 1988 series on the Chicago public schools.)

Sideline critics like me are quick to point fingers at the school board bureaucracy and at the Chicago Teachers' Union. It is noted that we provide the system plenty of money, enough so that the Chicago School Board spends about $4,000 per pupil each year, the same amount as is spent in Barrington, one of the nation's wealthiest suburbs. The fundamental problems lie deeper than in money for the schools. The schools with the "bottom one percent" rankings are imbedded in the social sicknesses of the areas they serve: poverty of money and spirit; absence of family, parenting skills, and good role models. One of my students at Knox College, a black from one of these schools, said the problem wasn't so much inside the classroom as in "getting through the gangs and into the schools each day."

Children with signs of potential are often "creamed off" to private or public "magnet" schools. Many of the remaining children are probably already lost to society before they enter first grade. Few Illinois leaders have really cared about the Chicago schools. Their children don't attend them, even if they reside in Chicago (only one of Chicago's 18 state senators had a child enrolled in a Chicago public school in 1988). The ghettos in which the worst schools are located are outside their field of vision.

So the bureaucracy and teachers union have done what organizational theorists would predict. As problems seem beyond fixing in the classroom alone, the teachers and staff have displaced the goal of good performance—which appears to them unattainable—with the pragmatic one of protecting themselves, with good pay and the privileges of seniority. They have done this through strikes, one strike every other year on average for the past two decades; some of the walkouts are long, like the 19-day walkout in the Fall of 1987.

I can empathize with the teachers. I would not take a job in the present system for three times what I make as a comfortable professor. I have come to think that we outsiders rather like having the bureaucracy and teachers to kick around, so as to deflect any blame from ourselves.

For those who seek something better than the public schools, a network of private school alternatives has developed, providing spaces for 126,000 pupils; 48,000 of these attend schools in Chicago operated by the Catholic archdiocese. The Catholic schools, many of which operate in the same slums as the worst-performing public schools, are often held out as models of what can be. According to Herbert Walberg and his coauthors, in a 1988 book about education reform for Chicago, Catholic schools report a dropout rate of one percent, versus about 50 percent for the public high schools. And 70 percent of the Catholic school graduates go on to college or further specialized training.

Public school teachers argue that the private schools are selective, do not have to take every child, and benefit from parents motivated enough to search out and pay for the opportunity. Even so, the Catholic schools achievement with poor kids is impressive. Walberg and associates credit the success to smaller, more personal schools, local school autonomy, and conscious choice by parents to send their children to the schools.

There have been many proposals for reform of the Chicago public schools. Among the most prominent ones: parental choice, increased authority for school building principals to hire and fire, and a breakup of the huge system into 20 or so autonomous districts. In 1988 the Illinois legislature wrestled with the problem. The lawmakers took steps that will achieve cosmetic, not fundamental, change. They created local school parent councils, and they gave the beleaguered principals more responsibility but without giving them any increased authority.

Even the more substantial changes I recommended earlier in this chapter would probably generate only marginal improvements in student outcome in Chicago, for education achievement is more heavily dependent on family, support groups, role models, and neighborhood values than on what goes on inside the classroom. We need view the education system as one of several elements that comprise a chemistry of community. The whole must be addressed simultaneously in Chicago and on a sustained basis if we are ever to graduate more inner city kids from high school with test scores closer to those of the suburban kids.

The Potential for Choice in Education

We come to accept old ways of doing things. For health care the tradition has been patient choice. We go to the doctor and hospital of our choice, and our insurance or government funding follows us. Though this has been changing for many persons enrolled in health maintenance organizations, choice is still the dominant model. Most of us would be outraged if we were told we could go only to the physician and hospital in our immediate neighborhood.

In contrast, monopoly rather than choice has long governed public school assignment. When a family contemplates a move, the first matter it checks out is likely to be the quality of the school district in which they might reside. It is accepted that there is no choice in the matter, unless the family pays tuition to place a child in a nonpublic school.

Momentum has been building since Ronald Reagan took office in 1981 to bring choice to education. Conservatives at the Heritage Foundation, the Hoover Center, and Manhattan Institute think tanks have been beating the drums, unsuccessfully thus far, for tuition tax credits and vouchers, so that families would have increased opportunities to select nonpublic elementary and high schools.

In the present monopoly, tax money is distributed directly to school districts. In a voucher model tax money would be distributed in "vouchers" to each parent of a child of school age. The voucher would go with the child to the school selected by the parent—either public or private schools in the pure form of the model—and the school could then redeem the voucher.

Though vouchers in the pure form have never been tried in the United States for elementary and secondary schools, the concept of choice has been around since before economist Adam Smith wrote *The Wealth of Nations* in 1776. Smith was a student at Oxford University in England in the 18th Century. He found that he studied virtually without supervision by any faculty and concluded that the professors were so comfortably endowed that they had no incentive to satisfy anyone other than their colleagues, as they had "the assurance of a budget independent of satisfied consumers." Thus was nurtured the idea of funding the student rather than the institution and of giving the consumer some leverage.

In fact, vouchers have been used successfully in many forms in the U.S., most notably via the G.I. Bill after World War II. Veterans enrolled at the public or private colleges and universities of their choice and federal government dollars followed them to pay for tuition and living allowances. There are other illustrations. In Vermont and New Hampshire there is a long tradition of school districts that do not operate their own high schools. Instead they pay tuition for youngsters from their district to attend public or private schools elsewhere.

This is still the case in Illinois in the few high school districts that do not belong to a community college district. Graduates of these high schools may go to any community college in Illinois and pay only the in-district tuition, while the sending high school pays an amount to cover the difference between tuition and actual college cost of education.

The biggest voucher program in the state is the Illinois State Scholarship Program. More than 100,000 students who have financial need receive grants to help pay tuition. The students may take these vouchers to any public or private college within the state (but not to for-profit institutions such as DeVry Institute of Technology in Chicago).

Vouchers offer one approach to choice; these two terms that are similar in concept—vouchers and choice—have become loaded into our minds differently, however, like welfare and the poor. Surveys have shown repeatedly that most Americans are against more money for welfare but are in favor of helping the poor. Voucher has a negative connotation for many, as it has been closely identified with efforts to provide public funds for parochial schools. On the other hand, most of us like the idea of having choices.

More important is the question whether vouchers or choice in some forms would improve the outcomes of our education systems. There are arguments against choice that impress me.

52 A NEW GAME PLAN FOR ILLINOIS

Many parents, especially the poorly educated, might lack knowledge of the choices available and could end up making bad choices. Wealthy school districts would draw pupils *and* financial support away from poorer districts, thus weakening the latter even further. With the government money might come increased government regulation. Writing in *Education Digest* in 1981, Laura H. Salganik summarizes concerns this way:

> Vouchers do not eliminate government control of education; they redefine it. Since funding is the ultimate mechanism of control, statewide voucher plans actually centralize government's role rather than reduce it, even if local public schools are retained.
>
> ... if vouchers are enacted during the next few years, that goal will probably be accomplished only for those with political power to control how education funds are spent. For many other families—regardless of whether they want alternatives—few options will exist; the only change will be that political control has been removed even further from their communities.

Going as far back as Adam Smith, the basic argument in support of choice is that there will be a powerful incentive to satisfy the customer that does not exist in a monopoly. Californians John Coons and Stephen Sugarman are leading proponents of choice in education. They contend that many positive consequences would flow from choice. Increased stability, for example, as choice would encourage some families who are satisfied with their schools to stick with them even after moving out of a school district. Schools would tend to develop specializations to attract students. A more professional relationship would develop between school professionals and parents because parents could exit a school and because parents would have the responsibility of choice.

For the most part, the assumptions of opponents and proponents are just that, for there has never been a major test of choice in our elementary and secondary schools. The nonoperating school districts in New England do not provide a good test, for there is no district public high school in the first instance, against which to evaluate the consequences of choice.

Minnesota is the place to focus our attention in the next few years. The state has enacted a policy that will allow a high school student to enroll in any *public* school in Minnesota, and the per pupil state funding will follow him or her to the district. In addition, 11th and 12th grade students have been able for several years to enroll in college courses at any public university or private college in the state, and their high school district pays the college tuition.

According to a lead article in the May 13, 1988 *Wall Street Journal,* these programs are having a powerful, generally positive impact on schools, students, and parents. Surveys show that parents whose children have switched to other schools tend to be more satisfied. Some schools are doing exactly what proponents of open enrollment predicted—adding courses and innovative programs to keep students. Governor Rudy Perpich notes that since the pilot program began in 1985 the number of foreign language courses offered throughout the schools has doubled. The college option is also popular. Four thousand high schoolers took advantage of it last year. Many are carrying full college course loads, and one Minneapolis high school alone has 200 students attending the University of Minnesota.

Though our familiarity with choice for all in education is limited, we have intimate understanding of the logic and consequences of both choice and monopoly in the broader American marketplace. Considering our preference for choice in the marketplace, it is amazing that taxpayers have stood so long for a system in which they pay heavy property taxes for education and yet get no choice whatever.

We hesitate to make change, however, because of interest group opposition and fear of the untested. I fear what we already have, especially in our urban public schools. In calling for vouchers, the *Chicago Tribune* editorialized on June 26, 1988:

> A voucher system is a drastic remedy. But Chicago's schools are dying and they are killing the futures of thousands of Chicago children—of the city itself. More than 300 studies on education reform have been done in the last five years in this country. But little has changed for children. The irreparable tragedy would be to make only a few cosmetic changes, throw in more tax dollars and pretend to have solved the problem.

I propose four policies to increase choice for students in Illinois schools and colleges:

* Authorize choice of districts for all students, within our public schools, as per the Minnesota plan. Close attention ought be paid to lessons being learned in the Minnesota "laboratory."

There will be all manner of issues thrown up to show why it cannot be done in Illinois, but it can be. For example, the state government in Minnesota provides much more financial support per pupil overall than do we in Illinois. This state support goes with a pupil to the school district he or she selects. The less state aid behind a pupil, the less attractive is choice to a receiving school district. This problem can be addressed by increasing per pupil state aid, as I propose in the chapter on state budgeting (see Chapter 8).

* Adopt also the Minnesota program that allows 11th and 12th graders to attend public or private colleges, explained above. Illinois has 187 college and university campuses, one or more within a few miles of almost every high school student in Illinois.

* Create a free market for all students among the 60 community college districts of Illinois. At present, most students who reside in one district must pay steep out-of-district tuition of $50-60 per credit hour to attend another community college, even though for many a campus in a neighboring district may be more convenient and more appealing. This would increase options for the many students who are somewhat mobile and increase competition among the colleges.

* Fund fully the successful Illinois State Scholarship Program for college and university students who demonstrate financial need.

As mentioned above, this longstanding voucher program provides tuition assistance to about 100,000 students in Illinois public and private institutions. For the past several years, however, state funding has been insufficient to meet all demonstrated need. As a result, about 20,000 students with need were denied aid. The students left out are from both middle-class as well as low-income families.

This full funding could be accomplished without an increase in total direct state appropriations for higher education. As ISSC tuition grants can be cashed only by Illinois colleges and universities, it all ends up with the institutions anyway. It makes more sense to fund students first, then institutions.

Untying Our Tongues

There is one element of education that is directly tied to

economic development: the ability to communicate—and sell—in the languages of other nations. In his book *The Tongue-Tied American*, U.S. Senator Paul Simon laments the pitiful inadequacy of foreign language training in our schools. He notes that foreign language teaching at our elementary-secondary schools reaches only one percent of our pupils. In contrast, Japanese pupils must take a second language, and for most it is English. The French require all pupils to take two foreign languages, at least four years of one and two years of another, beginning in the sixth grade.

Simon's book came to mind in 1987 when, of all things, I was robbed in Barcelona. Ironically, it was a good experience for me, like my Army experience. Let me explain. This was my tenth trip out of the U.S. in recent years. I was walking down a side street, away from an unfinished cathedral, a popular tourist site. A kindly-looking man, in his 50s or so, approached me to note there was ice cream on the back of my jacket.

What a mess. A youngster threw it, I thought. I stopped. The gentleman proffered help with a napkin as I twisted to survey the damage. Momentarily I put my briefcase down on a handy car trunk. *Voilá*! When I turned back the briefcase and the "kindly gentleman" were far down the crowded street. I gave chase, to no avail.

I reflected on what a clever deception this fellow had dreamed up, until I reached the police station. To simplify robbery reports, the police had printed a check-off list of common tricks, including "la mancha en la espalda," which they paraphrased—in English—as "the old ice cream trick!"

Es la vida! How was it good for me? I'm a little wiser and more experienced, with police stations, consulates, languages, on turf other than my own. And that is what we Americans need. More experience on turf other than our own. When traveling I notice that many fellow Americans appear uncomfortable, ill at ease. We are so comfortable and confident on our own broad U.S. landscape that we are shaken by our lack of self-assurance when on unfamiliar ground.

Yet our future is not on our own turf, as persistent huge trade imbalances testify; it is to be found on the Pacific Rim, in Europe, in countries with exploding populations. Our competitor nations have become experienced, self-assured on our turf, in our language, at our graduate research universities. For example, 48 of the 66 persons enrolled in graduate studies in statistics at the University of Illinois at Urbana in 1988 were foreign students.

We are in a struggle, no doubt about it. What to do? More foreign languages, much earlier. And required residence out of country for all college students, at the least for those in the liberal arts and business schools, as a requirement for graduation.

At present some colleges require a year or two of a foreign language. Too little, too late. Linguist Mario Pei points out: "The ease or difficulty of any language depends on the age of the person learning it. Before the age of 10, all languages are equally easy when learned by the natural speaking method (listening and imitating). After 10, our language habits are set in our own tongue.... Therefore, it is desirable to learn foreign languages as early as possible."

Colleges sponsor "study abroad" programs. More students are taking advantage of them each year, but still only a minor fraction of the whole. Many fail to benefit fully, because they have so little language preparation prior to departure. I propose that:

* Illinois vault ahead of other states—and simply join other developed nations—by providing 90 percent reimbursement to every school district that offers at least one foreign language from early grammar school through high school.

* Every public university in Illinois require a semester "abroad" as a condition of graduation for all students of business and the liberal arts. The rather modest additional cost of about $2,500 could be spread across eight semesters, to soften the cost impact and allow needy students to receive support through the state scholarship commission.

It is simplification to say "we can buy in English but we cannot sell in it," for English has become the international language of business and science. Nevertheless, by learning the languages of other nations and by living abroad for awhile, the coming generation of college graduates could develop deeper appreciation and sensitivity for the perspectives and values of people throughout the world. That increase in international understanding would help us develop and sell products for markets around the world.

Chapter 5

Economic Development

The 1980s have been a period of economic turmoil in the U.S. We endured a national recession in 1981-83, the onset of large, persistent national budget and trade deficits, and a dollar that rose to unprecedented strength and then plummeted. For national opinion leaders and public officials the buzz words became "economic development" and "competitiveness."

During much of this period I struggled as owner—and finally seller—of several community newspapers that operated in a rapidly declining rural setting, so I had a direct stake in the economy. I read many of the books that tried to explain what our economy has been going through. Most said our problems were cultural and systemic, rather than the result of specific governmental policies.

In *English Culture and the Decline of the Industrial Spirit*, historian Martin Weiner describes how the nation that created the industrial revolution lost interest in it, as sons of English industrialists yearned for the life of the gentry. He warns that we may be going through a similar process. Economist David Hale worries that "the huge concentration of people going into things like finance will make us a society good at administering wealth rather than creating it." Mancur Olson, another economist, observes that as nations mature they develop ever-more-specialized interest groups of business, labor, and agriculture that come to prefer protection over performance, production, and change.

In her compelling book *Cities and the Wealth of Nations*, Canadian urbanologist Jane Jacobs ties the decline of nations to the loss of creative capacity and to the lack of will of great city regions to generate "import replacement" goods for their regions. Jacobs added that conventional government economic development programs do more harm than good in the long term. She considers the billions of dollars pumped into Appalachia to have been counterproductive because the effort slowed necessary change and represented capital that could have been far more productive elsewhere.

She would say that giving money to people who do not really know what to do with it will not create wealth. If I read her correctly, she would oppose strenuously programs popular in the U.S. in which states offer big financial packages to attract foreign car manufacturers. This would simply be an admission of our own lack of creativity. It provides an international competitor with "beachheads" from which to expand its base later to its own parts supply manufacturers. And the profit generated flows back to the competitor for further investment. It is the opposite of Jacobs' import replacement concept.

These synopses are representative explanations by our more thoughtful observers, I believe. But when major economic problems slap us hard in the face, as in the '80s, we are too impatient to deal with the fundamentals. We demand that government do something, and be damned quick about it. (This strikes me as ironic, as surveys show that two in three Americans lack confidence in government to do the right thing.)

Public officials at all levels did respond with alacrity, and now we have 14,000 economic development agencies, councils, and committees in the U.S. Governments and their new agencies competed intensively for relocating businesses, with offers of enterprise zones, tax waivers, low cost capital, free land and buildings, and training grants. Many businesses moved; some from Illinois to Arkansas, some from Arkansas to Illinois.

During the frenzied 1984 bidding war for the General Motors Saturn plant, Governor James Thompson bragged that Illinois would beat the offers of any state, some of which were reportedly worth close to $1 billion. Tennessee, the state that won the prize, never even made a bid; it offered nothing, which suggests strongly to me that front-end sweeteners are of marginal importance. Illinois was selected more recently as the location for a new Chrysler-Mitsubishi auto plant. My friends in economic development say the decision was based as much on a

ECONOMIC DEVELOPMENT 59

Japanese strategy to locate at least one plant in each of the major Midwestern states—which has been done—as on Illinois' expansive package of financial incentives.

Some of the new ventures go sour. In 1988 Volkswagen announced that it was permanently closing its Pennsylvania plant, opened in the early 1980s, for which Pennsylvania had spent $40 million to outbid Ohio for the location. In the same year Heileman Brewing Company closed an old brewery in Belleville, Illinois, even though the state had earlier granted numerous concessions to keep the plant open. There are many similar illustrations. Clearly, we need to analyze the whole topic of net costs and benefits generated by state and local economic development programs.

My purpose in this chapter is not, however, to criticize programs aimed at economic improvement. They may have been quite valuable; they would have been pursued at any rate. You cannot ask Illinois to sit on its hands while Indiana and other midwestern states are out there bidding for new jobs. My purpose is to review where Illinois stands economically, what we have done, what we might yet do. For those who would like to go beyond my overview, the best source is the comprehensive collection of articles in *Economic Development in Illinois*, edited by Roy Wehrle and published in 1986 by *Illinois Issues*.

From 1975 to 1985 Illinois ranked near the bottom of all states in economic growth, ranking 48th in both manufacturing and non-agricultural employment growth and 46th in growth in aggregate personal income. Since 1987, however, Illinois and the Midwest have outperformed the nation's economy, led by rejuvenated exports and strong growth in the service sector.

As the editors of the 1987 *Illinois Economic Outlook* had predicted: "Increasingly, the attractive features of the state will reassert themselves." The key factors in any economy are markets, natural resources, transportation, capital, labor, and what I call the creativity and risk-taking quotients. Illinois is strong in the first four of these elements, but has severe deficiencies in its labor force (and in perceptions of it), and is anemic when it comes to creativity and risk taking. Let me review these briefly.

Sixty percent of the awesome U.S. market and a good part of that in Canada can be reached from Illinois in one day by semitrailer truck. Our natural resources would be the envy of any nation in the world. The Great Lakes states have been called, half seriously, the OPEC of water. One in every ten bushels of corn produced in the world comes from Illinois. Two thirds of Illinois is underlaid with coal; we have more BTUs of energy locked in our coal reserves than in all the oil under the hot sands of Saudi Arabia.

Chicago is the rail hub of the nation; it has the world's busiest airport in terms of passenger traffic. The city is the mail order capital of the nation and more telephone trunk switching equipment is located in the Chicago area than anywhere else in the world. We have probably the most complete network of interstate highways in the nation; Illinois has more miles of interstate highway (1800) than any state other than Texas and California, which have much larger land areas and are not so centrally located to the nation's markets. The Mississippi and Ohio waterways makeup our boundaries and they are linked to the Great Lakes by the Illinois River and canals.

Illinois is a net exporter of capital. Though our major Chicago banks are weaker today than a decade ago, the city is still a major money center. In 1982, the 26 venture capital firms headquartered in Illinois made $800 million in investments, but only $26 million went to Illinois firms.

When it comes to our labor force, however, we have several major shortcomings. I have already mentioned the albatross the whole state carries in having in Chicago "the worst school system in America." Our education achievement overall is mediocre, below average for the nation. For example, in percentages we rank 32d in adults who have completed high school, 31st in those of us who have completed some college, and 25th for those with four or more years of college.

On the plus side, we have large, strong colleges of engineering and science at several of our public and private universities. Unfortunately, in 1988 half the engineering students at the University of Illinois at Urbana planned to leave the state within the first year of graduation. In contrast, 90 percent of the scientists, engineers, and technical college graduates educated in New England remain in that area, as reported in *The Massachusetts Miracle*, edited by David R. Lampe.

There is much anecdotal evidence to suggest that Illinois

lacks a strong entrepreneurial culture that could make good use of those engineers who leave the state for careers elsewhere. According to John Talmadge of the Office of Technology Development at the University of Illinois at Chicago, the venture capitalists say they would rather invest here than on the coasts, but claim there are not many ideas here. Illinois inventors dispute this, but Talmadge points out, "You have to remember that venture capitalists have a fiduciary responsibility to make the best investments they can. We have a marketplace of competitive ideas, and I have a hard time believing that marketplace is warped somehow."

Talmadge thinks Midwestern conservatism dampens willingness to take risk. "What do you think the reaction would be to a guy who's 35 years old and making $60,000 saying he's leaving his job to form his own business?" he asks. "In Illinois, everybody says, 'You're crazy.' Everybody uses those exact same words. You make the same statement in Silicon Valley, and the response is, 'It's about time.'" Illinois venture capitalists interviewed by journalist Jeff Brody appeared unanimous that, while there were some venturesome, creative people in Illinois, there simply was much more entrepreneurial activity on the coasts and in places like Minneapolis.

I think it critical to Illinois' future that we do all possible to attract and develop more creative, risk-taking people, because of patterns of concentration that appear to be forming within new industries. For example, in Silicon Valley there is a critical mass of inventors, investors, product developers, and marketers. An inventor can walk down a single street in Silicon Valley and put together the team he needs to take his idea all the way to commercial distribution.

Brendan OhVallachain and James E. Peterson of Northwestern University's NCI Research say that economic development theory based on such conventional factors as transportation and cost of labor is becoming increasingly obsolete. They have found that fast-growing industries tend to cluster in established, generally urban settings. This reduces the costs of searching for talented labor, suppliers, distributors, research and information services.

They add that, based on their analysis of patterns of industrial growth, government policies of direct economic assistance and incentives seem to be of little consequence. So what have we been doing in Illinois?

Illinois' Response to Economic Change

The American states have added economic development to their list of functional responsibilities. Illinois is no exception. Governor James Thompson created a Department of Commerce and Community Affairs (DCCA) and staffed it with bright young men, most of whom had never met a payroll. They did what agencies do—they established programs to respond to every problem identified. There are programs for small business, large business, minority business, women in business, international marketing, tourism, business incubators, and movie development. At one time I counted 66 programs and initiatives in the department, most of them quite small, staffed by one or a few persons each.

The number of overseas offices was expanded to six, including the People's Republic of China, and at this writing an office is being readied in Russia. Consultants prepared a glossy five-year economic development plan that inventoried the state's strengths and deficiencies. It targeted "corridors of opportunity" throughout the state where economic growth appeared to have greatest potential.

The Governor became the self-proclaimed "top salesman" for Illinois. He has led Illinois trade delegations all over the world. After hearing his daughter repeat Michigan's tourism jingle, "Say Yes to Michigan," the Governor increased the annual budget for tourism promotion 1,000 percent in one year, from $1 million to $10 million.

All of this is fine, yet in perspective it is of marginal net value. Other states are aggressive in this arena as well. Minnesota governor Rudy Perpich bragged that he had been outside his state 120 days in one year, selling his state's economic strengths; the other big states have overseas offices also. Most of DCCA's budget represents federal not state funds for job training, community development grants, and energy conservation and assistance. These grants go to the other states as well. The state has committed more than $100 million from its "Build Illinois" bond fund for business loans and grants, but for fiscal 1989 DCCA

ECONOMIC DEVELOPMENT   63

projects it will make just 12 large business loans and 55 loans to small businesses.

There has not been a hard-headed evaluation of the net real value added that would not have been added without the increased state activity. I am confident there has been some, but in a state economy of more than $226 billion in annual product I am also confident the net increase in product and new jobs from state programs has been modest.

But I am quibbling. I would have done about the same things had I been governor, in order to reassure the citizenry that government was working for an economic rebound from a demoralizing recession and from a severe structural decline in heavy manufacturing jobs. The important question is what can be done by state government, if anything, that will contribute in a major way to development of a state economy that reflects the vitality found in Massachusetts and California?

What many of us failed to appreciate is that the seeds of the high tech success stories in those states were planted in the 1940s and '50s by a few creative people who were given support by other folks who were willing to take risks with their money. There was also a positive attitude toward spinning off laboratory ideas for commercial application on the part of two major private research universities, Stanford in California and Massachusetts Institute of Technology. After decades of pioneering work, these two high tech centers have developed critical masses of ideas, experience, and talented people who can rather easily put together the teams necessary for the development of additional ideas. (A non-scientist, I think of a critical mass as a concentration of elements so rich that it generates products that each element alone is incapable of producing.)

Illinois has no critical masses yet, but we have been taking steps to develop concentrations of ideas and talented people. One promising effort is the Biotechnology Research and Development Consortium (BRDC) centered around the U.S. Department of Agriculture's Northern Regional Research Center (NRRC) in Peoria.

The NRRC has been in business since 1940. NRRC scientists have many discoveries to their credit, including the method for mass production of penicillin, which laid the foundation for the antibiotics industry. A more recent one is called Super

Slurper, a form of corn starch that absorbs hundreds of times its weight in water and is now being used in products ranging from engine fuel filters to disposable diapers.

Corn starch is now being used to make biodegradable plastics for trash bags and drinking cups, and in a new process for taking harmful sulfur out of Illinois' high sulfur coal. Soybean oil is now being used in printing inks, and kenaf, a fast-growing bamboo-like plant, is being made into newsprint. Corn, grasses, and timber are being transformed into engine fuels that will someday replace petroleum fuels, as they have already in Brazil.

To increase cooperative biotech research activity and to enhance transfer of discoveries to business, Central Illinois Light Company put together in 1988 an unusual partnership of six major private corporations, the state and national governments, and several Illinois-based research labs. The companies include Dow Chemical, Amoco, and International Mineral and Chemical Corp. The labs include the NRRC and the University of Illinois Biotechnology Center. The companies will support increased research and develop commercial applications for promising laboratory findings.

Peoria congressman Robert H. Michel pushed legislation through Congress that would allow federal agencies like the NRRC to share its research with private enterprise more readily and to pursue new research in cooperation with them. The State of Illinois is contributing $4 million over four years, and the U.S.D.A. and the participating companies are making financial commitments as well.

L. H. Princen, director of the NRRC, has been disappointed that in the past so few U.S. companies have developed patents awarded to NRRC scientists. He puts part of the blame on U.S. business leaders who need to show profits too quickly, when it takes about seven years on average to transform an idea into a commercial product on the store shelf. Princen noted, for example, that 50 companies were approached for participation in the consortium before six, the number felt necessary as a minimum, were signed on.

The consortium structure and the investments made by the varied parties in this for-profit venture will increase interest in taking research off the laboratory shelf and into commercial development. The BRDC does not represent a critical mass, yet it could be the seedling from which the mass could develop over the years. Other logical research settings for the development of similar consortia are those at the several distinguished graduate research universities in Illinois, notably the University of Illinois, the University of Chicago, Northwestern, and Illinois Institute of Technology.

Higher Education and Economic Development
Higher education in the U.S. in the 20th Century has been characterized by quality, growth, and differentiation. So it has been in Illinois, which has one of the better systems of public institutions and many fine private colleges and universities. In 1940 Illinois could boast just one public university with 10,000 students and five teacher education "normal" colleges with about 2,000 students each. Today there are 700,000 students enrolled on 187 college campuses in Illinois; of these about half are students at our 50 public community colleges, where the average age of students is almost 29!

I have taught on six of these varied campuses and can tick off a long list of distinguishing features. In 1987 the college of engineering at the University of Illinois was ranked second best in the nation—which means in the world—after Massachusetts Institute of Technology. The former "normal" school at DeKalb has blossomed into a major national institution called Northern Illinois University; its accountancy program is one of the best in the nation, as are its programs in Southeast Asian studies and public administration.

At Knox College, the original ol' Siwash of old *Saturday Evening Post* stories, dedicated faculty work with students on a one-on-one basis. This stimulating environment contributes to the fact that Knox is a national leader in the percentage of graduates who go on to complete doctorates. Tiny Black Hawk Community College at Kewanee, where I taught in the evenings when I was a state legislator, has one of the best livestock judging teams in the nation and an equestrian program that draws students from 17 states.

Higher education is central to every element of our economy and its future vitality, from machine tool job retraining at Rock Valley Community College in Rockford to research into superconductivity at our graduate research centers. Yet the success of higher education in Illinois is hobbled by the inadequacies of the feeder system of our elementary and secondary schools. They simply are not producing enough graduates with preparation and inclination for study in engineering, math, and the sciences, which are the foundation for technological advances. As a result, our graduate programs in these fields are soon going to have majorities of foreign students. At present 58 percent of all doctorates in engineering granted by U.S. universities go to foreigners; the figure is approaching 50 percent in math and computer science.

Our need for top talent in these fields is going to become more acute in the late 1990s when there will be 25 percent fewer Americans of traditional college age than in 1988. According to the National Science Foundation, that could translate into a shortfall of 700,000 engineering and science graduates over 25 years. What good is it to have high quality universities if we are not meeting the fundamental responsibility to prepare our young people to take advantage of programs critical to our economic future?

I digress. Let me return to the linkage between higher education and economic development. In the 19th century the U.S. embarked on a massive, coordinated "industrial policy" that has proved successful beyond anything the Japanese have yet wrought. It was called the Morrill Land Grant Act of 1862 for development of public universities for agriculture and mechanics. In 1914 the U.S. government added farm extension programs to link the research—via itinerant teachers called extension agents—to the "quality circles" we call family farms.

As a student and later a faculty member at the University of Illinois at Urbana I walked by the Morrill Plots on my way home to my fraternity house or condominium. First plowed for research in 1876, this garden-sized plot of ground represented the first systematic agricultural experiment in the U.S. Now an historic site it is still used for research, and one can only marvel at the difference in productivity between the rows that are fertilized and cultivated well and those neglected rows at the opposite end of the small field.

I think we forgot the lessons of this partnership over the years, until our recent slippage in relative technological prowess. In 1977 the University of Illinois learned about the appeal of linking the university to economic development. Ron Brady, then the number two executive at the U. of I., took a flashy display over to newly-elected Governor James Thompson. It was titled Food for Century III and it called for major state investment in the College of Agriculture at the U. of I. to build a new ag engineering building, state-of-the-art greenhouses, and more.

Brady had simply bundled several projects the U. of I. was having trouble getting funded through the Illinois Board of Higher Education, and put a fancy ribbon around them, and labeled the bundle Food for Century III. It wowed the governor, because he and Illinois needed flashy economic development ideas like this, and he put the program in his budget. By 1988 all the projects for Food for Century III had been completed or were under construction. They comprise an impressive array of research labs and greenhouses that fill in the "south campus" at Urbana. There has not been enough time to discern if its promise is likely to be fulfilled.

We have been pinning much hope for an economic resurgence in Illinois on high tech companies that would spin off from university research. I attended a conference on this topic in 1985. It brought together academics, as well as bright young entrepreneurs who had indeed spun off. The academics had lots of ideas, while the entrepreneurs provided the important lessons.

The academics proposed a laundry list of stimulants: business incubators, venture capital funds, commercialization evaluation centers, entrepreneur-in-residence programs, new venture sabbaticals for faculty, and entrepreneurial education programs. There were discussions of the Michigan Research Corporation, the Indiana Center for Innovation Development, the University of Queensland Venture Fund, and University of Calgary Entrepreneurship Institute. All of which made it clear that everyone everywhere was into the game of higher education as economic development.

Yet the entrepreneurs were the most instructive, just in telling about themselves. Each of these fellows had taken his idea or new instrument out of the laboratory and started a new business. Many had created several new companies. Each was highly educated, with one or more PhDs, in fields such as physics, chemical engineering, computer science, and physiology. Each had an entrepreneurial spirit. They had been hustling since childhood. As one put it, while he and his friends all had paper routes, his had doubled in volume every six months.

These entrepeneurs would have spun off without incubators or innovation centers. They expressed caution about universities that would try to be something for which they are not suited. Pete Alsberg, an engineering physicist/computer scientist/businessman, put it bluntly: "Universities have survived because they stuck to their basic missions.... Universities decide slowly; entrepreneurs must decide quickly."

I drew a lesson from the conference. Universities should do best that which they can do: teach well and provide state-of-the-art research laboratories in which to nurture the creative, inquiring spirit. This will attract more of the best and the brightest faculty, some of whom will also be entrepreneurial by nature.

Daniel Alpert believes research universities also need to embark on fundamental reorganization if they are to make maximum contributions to commercial technological development. A physicist and director emeritus of the Center for Advanced Study at the University of Illinois at Urbana, Alpert presented a compelling paper on "Industrial Spin-offs from Universities" at the conference cited above. I summarize it here.

At most prestigious universities, including the University of Illinois, faculty are organized into specialized departments, such as electrical engineering, ceramics engineering, chemistry, and plant pathology. Peer review for purposes of faculty promotion and tenure tends to appraise the performance of a faculty member as an individual performer of research—as a loner. Alpert, who has worked as a research physicist in both industry and university settings, adds, "It mitigates against the individual whose output is inventions rather than papers, and whose personal style is that of making things work rather than learning why they don't."

It is not then surprising that most campuses, including the research campuses in Illinois, have had few industrial spin-offs, says Alpert. Stanford and MIT are cited repeatedly as the exceptions. They have the standard departmental structures as well, but they have had a much larger number of project-oriented, cross-disciplinary centers than other universities. The early spin-offs from these centers in the 1950s and '60s initiated the development of critical masses nearby of talented production, marketing, and business people who could help someone with a good idea bring it to market without requiring the creator to build his own team and factory.

Alpert concluded that the organizational experience of most universities, based on time-honored ways of running academic departments, is not suited to managing a mission-oriented laboratory. He recommends that research universities in Illinois be encouraged and supported in the establishment of mission-oriented research and development centers whose concern would be the industrial economy in Illinois and the Midwest. These centers would include faculty from many disciplines as well as substantial numbers of non-faculty engineers and other professionals. These centers would be complementary to the traditional departmental structures.

Alpert noted that the University of Illinois had not developed any such centers for 15 years, until the National Center for Supercomputing Applications and the Center for Supercomputing Research and Development were established in the mid-1980s. In 1988 the Beckman Institute for the study of human intelligence established a major new physical presence on the "north campus" of the U. of I. at Urbana. Funded by a $40 million gift from alumnus-scientist Arnold Beckman, this interdisciplinary center is the archetype of the Alpert model and is already proving to be a magnet that has drawn world-renowned scientists to its labs.

For the State of Illinois to fund additional research and development (R&D) centers would require a new approach to appropriating funds for higher education, which at present is done on a formula basis that is driven by student enrollments. Illinois needs to invest now in more mission-oriented R&D centers at our public and private research universities.

I propose that the state establish an Illinois Research Foundation headed by distinguished scientists and businessmen that would fund the best proposals. We must begin now in the expectation that one or more of the centers might one day spawn the critical masses of creative, entrepreneurial people and activity that do not exist in Illinois at present.

Illinois must also work harder to increase its miniscule share of federal R&D funds. By my calculations, these totaled about $32 billion in 1988. According to a 1976 study by William Brown of the University of Michigan, Illinois received less than two cents back in federal R&D funding for every tax dollar contributed to the national treasury. In contrast, California received 21 cents, Virginia 17, Massachusetts 16, and Maryland/ District of Columbia 31 cents.

The situation is even worse today. According to the Institute for Illinois, federal research and development obligations to Illinois have essentially been flat between 1977 and 1986, at less than $1 billion. In sharp contrast, R&D obligations for California have doubled, from $6 to $12 billion in the same period. Virginia also doubled its federal R&D activity, as Washington bureaucrats find it convenient to support R&D nearby, where they might work later, without having to relocate.

This is also confirmed by the miserable showing of Illinois in 1986 in R&D awards under federal Small Business Innovation Research (SBIR) set-asides. This is a program in which 1.25 percent of all federal R&D is set aside for small business. In 1987 Illinois received 49 SBIR awards worth $5.1 million while California garnered 759 awards worth $75.7 million. Massachusetts ranked second with 422 awards valued at $41.3 million.

This is intolerable because it solidifies the critical masses already in place in those states that get most of the funds, and inhibits congregation of creative people in states like Illinois. In addition to development of our own R&D centers proposed above, Illinois can also become more aggressive in making proposals for research funding. The State of Illinois has begun to provide assistance in this regard, through seminars and technical support in grant writing.

In an essay I wrote in 1985 I said there was something political parties, editorial writers, and community leaders could do about this funding imbalance—get nasty about it, *before* the next presidential election. "Instead of going hat-in-hand to a President after he is elected, when he can beg off by deferring to his bureaucurats, we must begin now to identify prospective 1988 candidates—when they are vulnerable—to pin them down for commitments to redress this R&D imbalance, with its longterm debilitating effects for states on the short end." I do think that

Governor Jim Thompson had this in the back of his mind during his hard work in behalf of former Vice President George Bush's presidential campaign, though it did not pay off in the case of the multi-billion dollar "super collider" project, which was awarded to Texas one day after the November 1988 elections.

Back home we need to review the structure and operations of our system of higher education, to see if we can increase the R&D activity without diminishing the quality of its other missions, all within a context of increasing competition for limited state funds.

The Challenge for Higher Education

James W. Carey is dean of the College of Communications at the University of Illinois at Urbana. He is most effective at reining in our expectations for university-related high tech. I quote this distinguished communications theorist at length because he writes so well and makes much sense:

> Despite our national penchant for founding a New Jerusalem or discovering a Passage to India, Americans take themselves to be a practical and hard-headed people. Yet, on the subject of high tech, a veritable rhetoric of the cybernetic sublime overtakes the calmest of minds and the most down-to-earth of our professionals, the engineers, I admire, I must admit, the audacity of it all, the sheer hucksterism, the renewed booster spirit, the evangelical fervor and enthusiasm with which this latest generation of machinery is promoted. . . .
>
> I am not trying to play the skeleton at the feast. One must give these proposals their due. The industrial activities represented by high tech are among the more promising opportunities for economic development now available. . . .
>
> (But) Everything a university can do about high technology can be done by technical institutes and research firms. The function for which there is no alternative is the scholarly one. That function includes the ability to stand apart, to be cool and inquiring and to take a longer view of the past and the future. That is the core of university life and the core of its teaching. . . .
>
> The point of this review is that the problems of higher education, as of the culture generally, go much deeper than and are not susceptible to cure by high technology. Indeed, what high technology principally offers is a new political coalition to shore up the otherwise declining support of higher education. . . .

The most important product of education is not knowledge, or service or education or a work force: It is the student.

Higher education in the United States—and in Illinois—is superior overall in its breadth, depth, and quality to that in any other nation. That is why students from Japan and the rest of the world crowd the corridors of our graduate research departments. According to *U.S. News and World Report*, in one recent year there were 101,000 foreign students studying engineering and the sciences in the United States, while only 2,600 Americans were pursuing those topics abroad. We must maintain this pre-eminence, but it will not be easy. Fortunately we can act now, before our superiority is challenged.

The public does not yet perceive a crisis in higher education, though tuitions have been rising more rapidly than inflation for eight years, and even though university presidents emit anguished cries when state funding falls short, as it has in Illinois the past three years.

The media have begun to pick critically at higher ed since about 1987, probably because leading editorial writers have been struck by the "sticker shock" of the tuition charges they face for their children who want to go to expensive East Coast schools. In my files I see a major piece by *Forbes* that doubts we are getting our money's worth in higher education, another from the *Wall Street Journal* that trumpets "exploding administrative costs on campus." Closer to home, the *Peoria Journal-Star* ran this headline: "Businesses watch their costs, but colleges just sock it to the students."

All the while, university leaders have been watching their share of state general revenue fund support decline, from almost 20 percent of the fund in 1969, the high water mark, to about 12 percent in 1987. And at the same time we have been asking higher education to do more in lifelong education, and in economic development, as I have done in this chapter.

The standard response is to seek increased state funding. Although as an erstwhile professor I believe the state ought to do all it can for higher education, the hopes of our university leaders in this regard will not be met fully in the years to come. Even in the event of a significant tax increase in Illinois in the coming year or two, a range of other claimants—some with needs even more compelling than those of higher education—will limit the gains for any one sector to rather modest increases.

For example, as noted earlier and often, only 11,000 of 112,000 poor children "at risk" are receiving early childhood services called for in the state's celebrated education "reforms" of 1985. It is estimated that $300-600 million a year in new money will be needed to provide a decent level of services for the mentally ill and disabled. Then there are the cost increases in health care for the indigent and aged. The list goes on.

So the key to maintaining superior higher education lies beyond the plea for more state money, and beyond next year's budget. With $1.4 billion in annual direct state funding alone, higher education in Illinois can be anything it wants to be, with distinction, but not everything.

We must determine what in higher education is best and most important, and then protect and build those elements. Unfortunately, we have political tendencies to do the opposite. In his 1985 book *The Zero-Sum Solution*, economist Lester Thurow noted that most states overbuilt their state universities in the 1960s. To protect the weaker campuses that are underenrolled he predicted that "The standard response will be to put enrollment limits on the popular state university campuses to force students to go to the unpopular campuses. . . .This is a policy of killing the best to save the worst. . . ." That is going on at present in Illinois, as enrollments have been cut back at the University of Illinois at Urbana and at Northern Illinois.

Ironically, the undergraduate popularity and reputations of campuses such as these may have little to do with the quality of the undergraduate programs. Dan Alpert says, "There is growing awareness of certain dissonances between the current practice of academic research and the undergraduate instructional mission." In lay terms he is saying that the undergraduate teaching mission is squeezed so as to make more resources available for the research mission.

It is the reputational rankings of the graduate departments and the visibility of faculty through their research work that generate the attractiveness of certain state university campuses, not the undergraduate teaching nor the level of direct faculty supervision of students. When I taught political science on the Urbana campus of the U. of I. in the 1980s, freshmen often took introductory American government and economics courses in classes of 1,000. Even my upper division courses would often enroll 130, far too many for close faculty-student relationships.

As a result, students were not asked to do much essay writing. In fact the College of Liberal Arts had to issue a directive that there be some kind of required writing assignment or essay portion of an exam, no matter how brief, in every course in the College. I write not to single out the University of Illinois, for which I hold great affection and respect. I simply point out what university administrators feel they must do to free time and money for faculty research, which is after all the basic mission of the Urbana campus.

These impressions of problems in higher education are presented to demonstrate that we need a thorough, independent review of our system of higher education. It has been 20 years since the last major outside evaluation. I propose an assembly of state leaders and national thinkers, patterned after the American Assembly of Columbia University, which would conclude with specific recommendations on how to maintain superiority in a context of limited state resources.

Here are suggestions I would offer to the panel.

1. Create a "triangle of research distinction" by making Northern Illinois University at DeKalb a part of the University of Illinois system. This would improve coordination among the Chicago, Urbana, and DeKalb campuses and reduce unhealthy program competition that has existed for the past decade. The points on this triangle would be within easy reach of two-thirds of the state population and of most corporate and non-university research laboratories.

2. Increase the role of consumer choice in identifying the most attractive public and private colleges. This could be done by increasing the amount of state funding that goes directly to students, and decreasing by a like amount the funding that goes directly to institutions. This could be accomplished by providing warrants to every student, or by funding fully the popular but underfunded Illinois State Scholarship Commission. The latter option would increase financial assistance for middle class but financially-strapped families.

3. Enhance the teaching role without diminishing the importance of research. Consider two tracks of professorships—

the professor of research (already in existence) and the professor of instruction, a track to reward and increase teaching productivity by exemplary classroom instructors. Related to this would be a shift of state budgeting for higher education from an enrollment-driven formula to one that makes separate appropriations for research and for instruction.

4. Increase cost effectiveness. This might be done via what I call "Alumni Panels on University Cost Effectiveness." Each of our public universities has successful business and management executives among its alumni. I am confident many of them would jump at the opportunity to participate in an intensive evaluation of the operations and systems of the ol' alma mater. Suggestions that would save $100,000 in annual operating costs would have more value than $1 million in additional endowment. And the alums would certainly not want to recommend anything that would harm their alma maters.

Even if the savings were relatively modest, there would still be the benefit of showing a positive, creative response to the calls from the outside for more accountability. We faculty like to put on our consultant caps, and march forth to tell all manner of enterprise how to do its job better, more efficiently. So why not have successful alums come in to look at how we operate?

5. Experiment with the concept of "higher education report cards." This idea was adopted a few years ago for our elementary and secondary schools, over the howls of school administrators. It appears, however, that the report cards have become valuable tools for comparison, used by parents, media, and school administrators. A report card for higher education institutions might provide standardized information on retention and graduation rates, placement services and success, average class size, and surveys of student satisfaction levels. This type of "consumer report" could prove valuable to parents, students, administrators, and public policymakers.

Governments are notorious for failing to act until a crisis has already befallen us, as in our belated efforts to reform elementary and secondary education. Here a crisis is brewing, at our colleges and universities, which we can prevent if we have the will and the creativity.

Summary

In this chapter I have touched on elements of fundamental economic development. My files contain folders stuffed with additional, intriguing ideas. For example, to train brokers who would match "low tech" manufacturers' needs for technology with the latest advances at our universities; establish a major Illinois department of international affairs that would coordinate all the state's international economic, educational, political, and cultural activities; and, eliminate the state income tax on capital gains from new companies.

These ideas may be valuable, yet they lack the importance of fundamental lessons from our nation's economic history. The breadth and quality of education are the foundation of economic prosperity. Partnerships between government (through research) and private enterprise have a long tradition of success. Critical masses of creators, researchers, entrepreneurs, and pools of skilled workers take decades to develop.

Chapter 6

To Help Every Poor Child

Half of Chicago's public high schools score in the bottom one percent of all high schools in the nation on standardized test scores. That is not, at heart, an educational problem; it is the result of deep social pathologies. Does the society of Illinois, working in part through its governments, have the knowhow, capacity, and will to transform that frightening statistic and all it represents?

I believe strongly the answer will determine the future of Illinois.

This is the chapter I kept putting off, out of anxiety that I could not fathom the problems, nor present a coherent, credible plan for making the transformation. But we cannot put it off. In this chapter I review briefly the core social problems that challenge Illinois. I offer proposals that I feel meet our social contract responsibilities and hold strong promise for reversing negative trends in key social indicators.

Neoconservative observers like Ben Wattenberg try to reassure us with statistics that things are not really so bad. He points out that high school graduation rates in the U.S. are higher than ever, that black youngsters are more likely to get a high school degree than was the case four decades ago. You and I are likely to live much longer than our parents, and infant mortality rates in the U.S.—and in Illinois—have been coming down steadily in the past decade.

It would be tragic, however, if we let those selected statistics serve as a balm for our consciences. The reality lies beneath those figures, in the shadows of black underclass ghettos, which Thomas Hammer calls "the negative space of black progress." The outlines of the underclass have become visible due to the departure of other blacks into the economic and social mainstream.

The tragedy encompasses a person as he drives the streets of East St. Louis, Illinois. The newsreel footage of bomb-gutted Dresden at the end of World War II comes to mind. Every other house is a burned out shell, or so it seems; the windows are empty, dark holes that stare back at you. Population has plummeted from 85,000 to less than 50,000 in three decades; half are on some form of welfare. The formal unemployment rate hovers around 20 percent, yet the statistic is a lie, for thousands gave up looking for work years ago and so are no longer counted.

Most of us never see or touch this all-black community that is located in a valley along the Mississippi River. The interstate highway whisks us over the town, from the bluffs in Illinois where the whites live, across the river to St. Louis. There is no reason for the traveler to stop; there are no motels or fine restaurants in East St. Louis. The Holiday Inn was boarded up years ago.

East St. Louis is walled off from you and me by the interstate, the river, the bluffs. In addition, there have been conscious, public decisions that cement these walls of separation. For example, when lines were drawn for the area community colleges, East St. Louis was carved out, leaving it an island that lacked either the population or tax base to support a jobs-oriented vocational college. (Under the late governor Richard Ogilvie, Illinois created and continues to fund the struggling State Community College of East St. Louis.)

People problems are not, of course, confined to urban ghettos. Only 40 percent of children in need are concentrated in our urban inner cities. And more whites than blacks are on welfare. As for teen pregnancy rates, yes, they are higher for blacks than for whites; however, a white teen-age female is twice as likely to give birth outside of marriage as in any other nation studied, according to Harold L. Hodgkinson of the Institute for Educational Leadership. He adds, "Every day in America 40 teenage girls give birth to their *third* child."

My 7th grade teacher retired recently after 40 years in the school rooms of a tranquil central Illinois farm town. I asked him what changes had taken place over the decades. "Jim, when I started in Toulon (Illinois, population 1200) it really stood out if there were one child in a classroom who came from a broken family. Now, in that same town of comfortable-looking white frame houses, there are so many we don't even bother counting them. Jim, family and community are breaking down."

The problems of people in Illinois need to be separated into at least two worlds. One is that of the underclass, a grouping of American "untouchables," whom we have abandoned psychologically to desperate, mostly black ghettos. The other comprises the rest of us, most of whom were brought up with middle-class values, but many of whom are struggling with problems in childrearing, health care, housing, and employment.

In this chapter I focus on the "untouchables" on the premise that we are defined by our attitudes toward the least among us. The underclass is a term for the permanently poor, many of whom we have consigned to high-rise housing projects that have become "free-fire" zones of violence for warring gangs. Most whites shun them as hopeless; many middle-class blacks have abandoned them.

The underclass has been chronicled repeatedly, in the *Chicago Tribune* (1986), and by Alex Kotlowitz in the *Wall Street Journal* (1987), among many. The descriptions belie reality; they numb us. Kotlowitz, describing the West Side of Chicago:

> When a friend of mine takes the elevated train home to Oak Park, a western suburb here, she makes a point of sitting away from the window. She worries she might get hit by gunfire while passing the Henry Horner Homes project.
>
> Pharoah Walton, age 9, lives in Henry Horner. For him, the shooting is so frequent and intrusive that he's learned over the years to look both ways before running when he hears gunfire.
>
> Our inner-city neighborhoods, particularly public housing projects, have become islands of violence, isolated both geographically and in spirit from the rest of us. Delivery trucks and taxis dare not venture into these embattled neighborhoods, which are cordoned off by boulevards and highways.
>
> When the apartment next to the Waltons was firebombed this fall, there was no public outcry. No political leader came forth to say that this must stop. The news media didn't run major stories on the terrorist attack. The police didn't come out in full force. Even the local residents took it in stride. In the jargon of Henry Horner, just another apartment was "cocktailed."
>
> ... There is, say residents, a feeling of terrible aloneness.

Most disturbing, however, is how little we know or care about what happens on these inner-city reefs. Most of us are like my friend, for whom the neighborhood is a blur and the violence a momentary but passing threat.

We are allowing a "third world" nation to take root in the heart of our cities. Many developing nations would not tolerate the daily violence of our projects. I feel more secure in the poorest parts of Guadalajara and Mexico City than I do driving by the Cabrini-Green public housing project that is just a stone's throw from Chicago's gilded "gold coast" of luxury high-rises. (I was told by someone who ought to know, but I cannot confirm, that one-half the young men born into Cabrini-Green are either in prison or dead by age 18.)

The underclass ghettos have direct consequences for all of Illinois. We are home to the nation's largest black ghetto, with dimensions of eight miles by four miles, on Chicago's South Side. Add projects like Horner and Rockwell Gardens to the west, and Cabrini-Green on the near northwest and you have a noose, or albatross, draped around the proud, tall Chicago Loop.

The well-chronicled existence of this underclass sends messages loud and clear to all the world as to what we in Illinois allow, of what we are about, and of what our skill and education levels are not. The *Chicago Tribune* editorial of March 27, 1988 was titled, "The saddest story of the week." It told that 2,500 of 4,000 summer jobs made available by private employers went unfilled in 1987 because most of the applicants—and there were more than enough—could not read, write, or compute well enough to handle the simple, beginning-level positions. Many of them even had high school diplomas from the Chicago Board of Education.

The inner-city has always been a difficult place; now it is a harrowing, deadening place. William Julius Wilson is a black professor of sociology at the University of Chicago. He points out that: "Despite a high rate of poverty in inner-city areas during the first half of this century, rates of joblessness, out-of-wedlock births, single families, welfare dependency, and crime were significantly lower than they are today and did not begin to rise rapidly until after the mid-60s."

Nicholas Lemann wrote a series on Chicago's underclass for

Atlantic Monthly in 1986. He notes the deterioration in the ghetto, quoting a black who moved from Louisiana to the Cabrini-Green project in 1956. "I remember very vividly getting off the train at Twelfth and Michigan and being picked up and taken here. It seemed like Shangri-la." Lemann continues:

> Cabrini-Green was then all low-rise, and it housed many Second World War veterans and their families, both black and white. Today it is mostly high-rise and all black. The population of the high-rises is as much as 75 percent poor and 65 percent are under twenty-one and 80 percent are in female-headed families. The project has virtually no church attendance or legitimate business activity. The high school that serves it has a dropout rate of 89 percent. Four major gangs and close to a hundred subfactions are active there.

This, in the shadows of the Loop, and in the wake of the great federal War on Poverty!

Journalist Lemann describes a process that has played a major role in shaping the underclass. First, the migration of rural blacks to the north, followed by the more recent migration of middle-class blacks out of the ghetto. This has resulted in social disorganization and masked the deterioration for those left behind. According to Lemann, descendants of black sharecroppers are less likely to have made it in the North than black kids from town, whose parents tended to be more self-sufficient. He finds striking similarities between the socioeconomic systems of sharecropping and public welfare systems of today, both of which create a dependency on "the man," or the "welfare office."

The civil rights movement of the 1960s was beneficial for middle-class blacks, who were prepared and motivated to take advantage of job opportunities, and of newfound housing mobility. As a result, these good role models with their middle-class values fled the ghettos, leaving little behind. For Lemann the problems of the underclass are anthropological and cultural, not basically economic.

Sociologist Wilson accepts much of the Lemann thesis but casts the problem primarily in terms of economics and job availability. He points out that the "marriageable pool" of men (men with jobs or decent prospects of jobs) is much smaller for blacks than for whites, especially among young blacks. For example, in the North Central U.S. (which includes Illinois) the pool of marriageable black men age 16-19 is only 25.5 per 100 black women, and the rate has been declining. The rate for whites is more than double that for young blacks. He sees a strong tie between the disintegration of poor black families and black male prospects for stable employment.

The problem is not initially the innocent child, but his or her home environment. Census data on births for 1986 show that half of all the black women who had a baby were not married. Neither were 23 percent of Hispanic mothers or 12 percent of whites. Three of five of the unmarried mothers were under 25. A majority of unwed mothers must turn to welfare for support (55 percent of all children born out of wedlock in the U.S. in 1980 were receiving Aid to Families with Dependent Children in 1981), and their average period of dependency is more than nine years.

More than 70 percent of poor black families are headed by unmarried women. In contrast, more than 80 percent of "intact" black families (those with both husband and wife present) live above the poverty line. Senator and erstwhile professor Daniel Patrick Moynihan (D-New York) says, "the stability and quality of family life are a prime determinant of individual and group achievement." He continues:

> There is one unmistakable lesson in American history: A community that allows a large number of young men to grow up in broken families ... never acquiring any stable relationship to male authority, never acquiring any set of rational expectations about the future—that community asks for and gets chaos. Crime, violence, unrest, disorder ... are very near to inevitable.

The chilling aspect of Moynihan's now prophetic observations is that they were made 25 years ago in an article that he hoped would provide a clarion call for national action. Did we as a society not listen, not heed, not know how to respond? What have we been doing about the problems of poor children and their oft-broken families? What ought we do?

Lemann says—get them out of the ghetto. "The negative power of the ghetto culture all but guarantees that any attempt to solve the problems of the underclass *in the ghetto* won't work— the culture is too strong by now. Any solution that does work, whatever it does about welfare and unemployment, will also have to get people physically away from the ghettos." Wilson says—get them jobs. And do so by intervening early in the lives of underclass children, and stay with them all the way to the jobs.

Options for the Future

In a 1986 essay I proposed the following, after I had laid out the desperate problems of East St. Louis:

> I say let's be bold, let's take a gamble on East St. Louis, its Mississippi riverfront property and Heartland location. Let's build a four-star, state-owned-and-operated casino . . .
>
> By its nature, the operation would tend to attract those from middle-and high-income strata of society . . .
>
> I propose that the net income be dedicated to East St. Louis. Rather than try to rebuild a city that was once based on m a n u - facturing and butchering, I would focus the revenues on transition programs for the young. There could be nurturing and education programs that could start before birth and carry on through high school.
>
> Bluntly put, I would provide youngsters the tools by which they could leave East St. Louis for productive lives elsewhere, or stay, should opportunities develop at home.

Friends and associates who read the newspaper essay were either bemused or offended by the idea of using a distasteful enterprise to attack a social problem. So I said, "Okay, it's a lousy idea. What's your proposal for East St. Louis?" To a person, they shrugged—the old "throw up your hands in futility" syndrome. That is not good enough. Since then I have investigated the spectrum of policy options that we have for attacking problems like those in East St. Louis. I have even shaped a couple more of my own.

There is no shortage of demonstration programs in progress. The National Governors' Association has published a kind of cookbook of early childhood programs that are percolating in the laboratories of federalism that we call the states. *The First Sixty Months* describes 19 programs, from the home instruction program for preschool youngsters in Arkansas to the "homebuilders" family preservation program in Washington State. The Committee for Economic Development, a prestigious national group of business executives, published a similar glossy booklet in 1987 titled *Children in Need*. Their report trumpets a similar listing of early childhood intervention programs that are working. The business leaders conclude that a dramatic increase in our investment in poor kids is imperative if we are to meet the economic challenges of the next century.

The simple pyramid at Figure 6.1 identifies the basic stages of social problem development. Thus far Illinois state government has generally stepped in only when the problem has become severe. State government has traditionally played an "institutional" role, as with mental hospitals and "schools" for the retarded, and children's "homes," and prisons.

Figure 6.1. Plateaus of intervention.

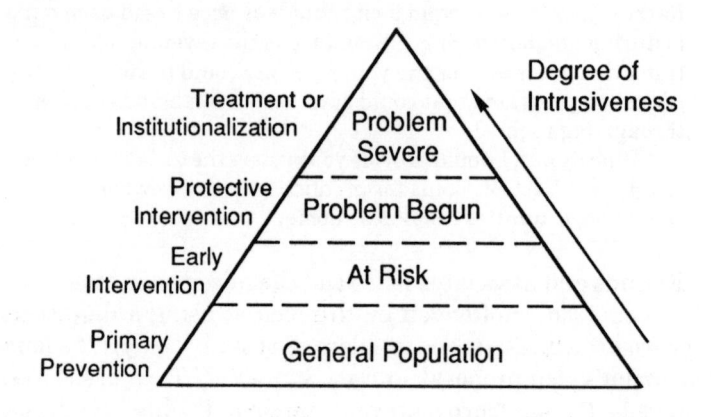

```
                          /\
                         /  \         Degree of
       Treatment or     /    \ ←      Intrusiveness
   Institutionalization/Problem\
                      / Severe  \
           Protective/-----------\
         Intervention/ Problem Begun\
              Early /----------------\
       Intervention/     At Risk      \
            Primary/-------------------\
         Prevention/  General Population \
                  /─────────────────────\
```

Source: National Governors' Association, *The First Sixty-Months*, July 1987.

By the time a problem is severe, it is often too late to turn matters around. A survey of Illinois and other big states found in 1987 that seven of every ten prison parolees age 17-22 are re-arrested for serious crimes within six years. That does not include those who may not get caught! In recent years there has been an effort to shift from care in massive state institutions to care in community-based facilities and programs. Still the focus has been on persons with severe problems.

The Illinois Department of Children and Family Services

(DCFS) spends $100 million a year for 10,000 youngsters who need "substitute care," that is, foster families or institutional homes. Clearly these youngsters faced severe problems, such as abandonment or continual abuse. That same department spent only $250,000 in 1988 on efforts to preserve families that have begun to show signs of possible breakdown that would result in children coming onto the state rolls.

DCFS caseworkers are each assigned 50 or more families with whom to work in trying to keep parent(s) and children intact. That works out to about 1/4-day a month per case family, which is not enough time to do the paperwork, let alone provide any counseling or support for the problem families.

Help for Every Poor Child

It is time to move beyond small pilot programs to a fundamental commitment to the half-million children in Illinois who are on welfare. Our objectives ought to be that we get each child under five as close as possible to the same starting line for formal education as the line for typical middle-class children. To do this requires good nutrition and health, stimulation about the larger world around the child, and a positive, self-confident attitude toward the future. These early months are not only formative but in large part determinative of educational success and adult outcomes. The public must be conditioned to the fact that it will require almost a generation of effort before results are seen.

There are many constructive ways in which to provide the early childhood support. Here are several basic approaches, two of which are in use for some children already, plus a radical proposal to resettle ghetto families.

1. The Wisconsin Child Support Assurance Program. This program overcomes the deficiencies of conventional court-ordered child support programs, which have been characterized by high rates of payment delinquencies, uneven levels of child support, as well as by anguish, uncertainty, and often poverty for the custodial parent.

Wisconsin has established a minimum child support level. Each child in a single-parent family for which the court has ordered noncustodial parent support is guaranteed to receive promptly the minimum child support level or more. This is accomplished from the child support payments, custodial parent income, the state, or a combination of these sources.

There is immediate income withholding of court-ordered support payments (which has also been implemented in Illinois as of 1989). If for any reason these required payments are not forthcoming, the state makes payments up to the minimum child support level.

2. A Beethoven Project for Every Underclass Child. This is a nationally-acclaimed program of intensive early childhood and parent support for young families in the Beethoven Elementary School enrollment area. The school serves children from six of the 28 buildings of the Robert Taylor Homes, the nation's largest public housing project. Every child is provided developmental programs that begin with prenatal care for the mother and continue through age five, so that these children will come close to the same starting line for schooling as children outside the ghetto housing projects.

The program is the brainchild of businessman-philanthropist Irving Harris and is supported by the Urban League and state and federal governments. It works within a circumscribed community using community people for whom intensive training is provided. I propose that this program be adopted, along with lessons learned thus far, throughout the underclass ghettos of Chicago and Downstate cities.

3. Meeting the Basic Standard of Need for All Poor Children. Children comprise two of every three persons in Illinois in the federal-state program of Aid to Families with Dependent Children (AFDC). Illinois provides an AFDC family cash and noncash benefits such as food stamps that in total meet only 79 percent of the "Illinois Standard of Need," the minimum living standard determined necessary for health and well-being by the state (which in turn is only about 80 percent of the federal poverty level established by U.S. Department of Commerce).

I propose that Illinois meet at least 100 percent of the minimum living standard the state has established, inasmuch as most of the recipients are children. This would require about $400 million in additional annual funding. The national government would contribute half the amount, as it matches state funding for AFDC on a fifty-fifty basis. I would require that parents participate in education and job training programs in return for this increased support.

4. One Church/One Family—A Ghetto Resettlement Program. This represents a radical proposal to take many of the underclass out of the ghetto by resettling single parent families with churches throughout Illinois. It is based on three successful programs. One is the U.S. refugee resettlement program that has been active since 1975. The second is the One Church/One Child program in Illinois in which black church congregations adopt black children.

Third is the "Gautreaux" program in metropolitan Chicago, named for the plaintiff in a 1976 fair housing case who charged improper segregation in public housing in Chicago. Since then a housing group has plucked some 3,500 families, mostly black and headed by a single parent, from housing projects and transplanted them to private, rent-subsidized suburban apartments. Gautreaux families are moved by ones and twos into existing housing, where neighbors are unaware of their backgrounds. It has been tough on the mothers, who sacrifice friends and extended family to make the moves. Yet the sacrifices have paid off for the children, according to a Northwestern University study team, that found the transplanted youngsters are meeting higher academic standards in their new settings.

Several premises undergird my proposal. First, people do not like living in hell holes and we ought to be helping these people out. Second, this is exactly what people have been doing when they could. The Woodlawn area of Chicago has decreased in population from 81,000 in 1960 to about 30,000 today; East St. Louis had 80,000 in 1960 and fewer than 50,000 today. Those left behind are those who cannot escape, for lack of money, education, and self-confidence. They need help. Nicholas Lemann contends these people probably cannot be helped much where they are, embedded in a profoundly advanced pathology of social disorganization and decay, and lacking effective community support and leadership elements.

We have been resettling people successfully since before Jane Addams set up Hull House in Chicago in the 19th Century. In recent years the U.S. government, church groups, and community volunteers have teamed up to help hundreds of thousands of Vietnamese, Ethiopians, Hmong tribesmen, and others re-establish themselves in our country. One of the most effective of these partnerships is located next door in Iowa, where the Catholic Diocese of Davenport has worked with Presbyterian and other church congregations to resettle more than 3,000 refugees since 1975.

In June 1988 I interviewed Betty Anderson, the director of this program, and Alice Spuller, her chief volunteer. The refugee program works like this. The U.S. Department of State provides refugee families a six-month training program in the English language and in American ways before the families come to the United States. The State Department contracts with not-for-profit organizations like the Catholic Diocese of Davenport to assist in resettling families. The local units develop networks of churches of varied denominations that volunteer to "befriend" individual refugee families.

The State Department allocates a small amount of cash assistance for each family, which is distributed by the local program director. This amounts to $200 or so per family member. Refugee families are eligible for the same social welfare programs as are U.S. families, such as the medical assistance "green card" and food stamps. Local "befrienders" help find affordable rental housing and scrounge among parishioners for furnishings and other basic items needed.

Refugee families are assisted intensively for the first six to nine months, after which the program director tries to wean families away from dependency, though a typical family is in active communication with the resettlement program for about two years.

There is only one fulltime paid staffer in the Catholic Diocese of Davenport program, the director Betty Anderson. According to Anderson, the keys to success in resettling a family are these: the desire of a family to make the move; the quality of the preparation of a family for the transition prior to the move; active volunteer befrienders from a local church, and a support group of families of background similar to that of the resettling family.

In One Church/One Family I propose that the State of Illinois enlist active assistance from among the approximately 12,000 local church congregations in Illinois to "befriend" single-parent families from the poorest underclass ghettos of our state, in much the same way that we have resettled refugee families from other nations. There would be little new money involved, as the families would take with them whatever social welfare assistance they had been receiving.

The keys would be to identify families that were motivated to leave the ghetto, prepare families for their moves, and contract with local or area groups such as a diocesan social service unit to provide local arrangements and a network of volunteer befrienders. I would try to steal Betty Anderson away to help organize the program, and I would call on tough, savvy, capable Sister Julia Huiskamp of the Catholic Urban Programs of East St. Louis to develop the local identification and preparation elements.

There are daunting difficulties with the proposal. It might be challenged as inherently racist, as the concept calls for placing thousands of families, mostly black, in new surroundings, mostly white. The cultural chasm between an urban black family and, for example, a farmtown Methodist congregation is thought to be enormous. Yet so is that between a black Ethiopian family and an Iowa church group, and between non-English-speaking Laotian refugees and Midwesterners.

Yet if half the state's 12,000 congregations would each befriend small groups of single-parent families every two years, we could begin to transform the social arrangements of Illinois. It is what I call a "transforming idea" because it confronts us at home, in our own parish or congregation, to fulfill our basic Judeo-Christian values as well as our American ideology of providing every child something close to an equal opportunity at the starting line of formal education.

Short-term and Long-term Benefits

Public officials feel a need to show benefits rather quickly from expensive or controversial programs. Otherwise how can they justify putting their voters through the sacrifice involved? In this chapter I have offered expensive and controversial proposals that will not show benefits for years. Yet I contend there are dramatic short-term indirect benefits for Illinois, *if* we proceed with a total commitment not just of financial resources but also with the personal involvement of the community of Illinois.

If we can find the will to transform ourselves in order to

achieve the basic yet profound goals set forward in this chapter, then we will also transform the way in which the world sees us and the way in which we see ourselves. There can be no greater benefit.

Chapter 7

Images and Realities— The Creative Arts, Our Natural Resources, and Rural Illinois

This chapter presents my observations about three diverse elements that have been central to the quality of life in Illinois. The images and realities of these elements also tend to diverge. The creative or fine arts flourish in Illinois yet are underappreciated and inadequately presented to the world beyond Illinois. We have an abundance of natural resources yet they are under great pressure. Much of rural Illinois is gripped by deep economic distress that is out-of-sight to most other Illinois residents.

I think of quality of life as those elements one prizes for oneself and one's family, those elements of life that sustain, reassure, and stimulate us. They include economic opportunities, the environment, schools, housing, sense of safety and well-being, the arts, cultural and recreational amenities, and others you would add to this incomplete list. A 1977 survey for the Rand Center, a policy research group, identified quality of life as the single most important variable in business location, more important than factors such as taxation or unionization. Since then I have seen numerous economic development plans that emphasize the importance of developing quality of life, and state and community promotions that trumpet the high quality of life to be found in their backyards.

Minneapolis and St. Paul have higher taxes and harsher winters than do we in Illinois, yet many creative folks and business executives desire to locate there, in large part because they perceive a rich quality of life overall. Pittsburgh, that sooty town of earlier image, was named the most livable city in the U.S. in 1985, based on some twenty-two variables. Pittsburgh won primarily because it was ranked very high in the areas of public education, the environment, and the arts.

How do we know what quality of life exists in a place where we have not lived? We imagine it. In 1984 the *Chicago Tribune* lamented that a survey by the Commercial Club of Chicago found that chief executives nationwide gave Chicago a poor rating as a city to locate new business. The survey revealed, however, that the attitudes of outsiders were based more on image than on reality. Those surveyed thought that crime rates and taxes were higher than they actually were, and they knew little about Chicago's cultural assets.

The late political observer Walter Lippmann wrote that each of us sees the world through the pictures or images we develop in our heads. These mosaics of the mind are always incomplete and to some extent distorted. There are five billion or so people in the world. We in Illinois comprise less than one-quarter of one percent of that total. What are the pictures or images that the rest of the world conjures up for Illinois?

Most persons outside this country have no image or picture whatever of Illinois. When traveling outside the U.S., downstaters and suburbanites generally find it necessary, grudgingly, to cite Chicago before a glimmer of recognition is achieved. We have heard it often, yet it is still the case that many around the globe have outdated, unflattering pictures of Chicago. On a recent trip to Mexico I turned on my hotel room television during prime time to find Elliot Ness still chasing Frank Nitti up North Clark Street.

We have tried advertising campaigns to boost tourism and to develop a positive statewide image. In my memory we have been the "Land of Lincoln," the "Tall State," and even two states—as in "just outside Chicago, there's a place called Illinois." More recently we tried to convince people, including ourselves, that we're in a "Happy State." With the possible exception of the "Land of Lincoln" connection, these campaigns have failed. They have been ephemeral, here this year and gone the next, and they have failed to capture what we in Illinois are about, probably because we are not sure ourselves.

We ought not be misled by the idea that we can shape a

lasting image for Illinois in the creative shop of an ad agency. The job for our leaders is to promote realities where deserved, and to change realities that shame us. As I have said before, Illinois has to make a deep, lasting, and costly commitment to our children, especially our poor children—our human capital. If we fail in this, the reality of the stark contrasts between the shimmering brilliance of new skyscrapers and the shadows they cast over depleted ghettos will tarnish our image forever.

It is okay for governors to fund advertising campaigns. These may boost tourism and even help our image at the margin, yet they represent surface not substance. Leadership is about something much different. It is about lasting commitments to the building and changing of realities.

Quality of Life for the Creative

As noted in Chapter 5, I subscribe to the Jane Jacobs thesis that economic prosperity tends to develop in environments that attract and retain creative people and that foster their creative activity. These people have ideas about new, better ways of doing things, plus the self-confidence and drive to work to see their ideas developed. My evidence to support the thesis is based on admittedly unsystematic observations. The greater San Francisco Bay area and metro-Boston would be my prime illustrations. They both have critical masses of these types of folks.

Creative people comprise a minute fraction of the whole of us. I think we Americans are distributed in a somewhat normal or "bell shaped" curve configuration when it comes to our skills and creativity. Most of us are worker bees who labor rather unimaginatively for family and community. The quality of our toil and our work habits are important, certainly, yet we labor at the inventions and discoveries of a handful of people and through the financial risks taken on these inventions by another small group of creative capitalists.

If you have taken an elementary statistics course—as far as I got—you might recall that about 95 percent of us are within two standard deviations of the mean and 99.73 per cent of us are within three such deviations. The really creative contributors are probably in that tiny fraction of us located outside the positive end of two or even three standard deviations on the bell-shaped curve.

I dwell on this not because I am an elitist who believes these few are better than the rest of us just because they are more richly endowed on this dimension of creativity. I do so because I think it makes sense for the longterm wellbeing of all of us that we consider what qualities of life are of compelling attractiveness to these rather mobile creative and risk-taking folks.

The visual and performing arts comprise a critical component in defining quality of life for creative people. I could see this clearly during my years on the faculty at the University of Illinois at Urbana-Champaign. The broad foyer leading to the several theatres of the Krannert Center for the Performing Arts was filled each evening with distinguished faculty from all academic disciplines.

The arts are appreciated by a much wider spectrum of people, of course, including business leaders. According to a survey reported in the July 1988 issue of *Governing*, the state of the arts in a community is among the top six—and sometimes the top three—questions that corporate relocators ask. And, maybe even more important in the long run, arts activities are appraised continually by international media observers, the people who define the images and perceptions that people around the world have of metropolitan areas.

Illinois residents have long enjoyed great richness and texture in the arts, superior to all other U.S. states with the exceptions of New York and California, I would guess. Unfortunately, this has been one of our best kept secrets, something most of us who live here underappreciate. In recent years there has been more effervescence in the Illinois arts than in a vintage magnum of Dom Perignon.

Illinois is second among the states in the number of residents who identify themselves as artists (in all disciplines), according to the Bureau of the Census. Sparkling recent additions to the Chicago cultural scene include the Chicago Art Exposition, already one of the world's leading juried art shows; the Chicago International Theatre Festival, and the New Music Chicago festival, which showcases the diversity and explorations of Chicago and Illinois composers. Chicago's River North district, once characterized by dilapidated factories and warehouses, has become a visual arts center compared favorably with New York's SoHo district.

There are about 100 theatre companies in the metro-Chicago region. Wisdom Bridge, Steppenwolf, and the Goodman theatres are receiving plaudits worldwide. Downstate the Illinois Shakespeare Festival at Ewing Manor in Bloomington has marked a decade of distinguished performances. In Champaign-Urbana impresario Roger Shields is developing the Stravinsky International Music Awards, which have been attracting young musicians from every continent. Mt. Vernon (pop. 17,000) in southern Illinois is home to two major arts attractions—the Mitchell Museum, with its collection of prominent 19th and 20th century paintings, and the annual Cedarhurst Chamber Music series, featuring performances by international and local talent. The list goes on.

Illinois must learn how to market this arts richness for all the world to know—and for us to appreciate fully—as proof positive of the high quality of life in Illinois. I have proposed, for example, that we create the Illinois International, an annual, month-long celebration of the visual and performing arts. Noted artists from throughout the world, and especially those nurtured in Illinois, would be invited to perform with our own renowned symphony, vocal, and dance ensembles. There could be competitions, premieres of works by Illinois composers, and master classes. Community arts groups and artists would join fully with the professionals in this celebration. One year the Illinois International might be resident on Chicago's lakefront, the next at the Krannert Center in Urbana, and then on to Evanston.

Another idea of mine has been to establish the Voice of Illinois, a fine arts network supported by the state that would produce high-quality video and audio programming for distribution throughout the world, including performances from the Illinois International. WFMT is a Chicago fine arts radio station that beams live programming around the world. The station has developed a national program service called the Beethoven Satellite Network. This might provide a model for the concept. Over the years, the signature of the Voice of Illinois could come to trigger immediate positive pictures of our cultural endowment and quality of life.

These ideas by this non-artist, who could never move up from "last chair" in the alto sax section of his rural high school and municipal bands, may not be practicable as sketched here. The ideas are less important than the imperative that we develop a strong, positive arts "signature" for Illinois for all the world to identify. After all, this represents a longstanding reality in Illinois. A sage friend of mine observed wryly that "the arts aren't for everyone, just those who create and those who determine where to locate their businesses." The arts are for everyone, of course, yet there is import in what my friend says.

There are many resources that define quality of life. In addition to education and economic elements that I tried to address in earlier chapters, there are the natural resources— and our stewardship of them.

Stewardship of Our Natural Resources

I first draped myself in the mantle of a steward of the good earth for political reasons, I must admit. There had been much stripping of rich farmland for coal in the counties that lay in and near the state legislative district for which I sought a House seat in 1966. Farmers were against the stripping. The scars of barren, moonscape-like stripped land were evident from the car window as one drove across the flat or gently rolling central Illinois countryside that was otherwise planted to corn and soybeans. In my district Henry County proclaimed itself, as it does today, the Hog Capital of the World.

Most of the land in my old district is underlaid by reserves of commercially-strippable coal, and there were fears coal companies might destroy the patrimony of our region. So it was a win-win issue for this fledgling young politician. Soon I became a believer as well. The coal operators were not bad guys, just capitalists trying to maximize return on investment, though we sketched them in black hats and pencil thin moustachios when we described those bad guys far away in their corporate boardrooms. After all, they did strip off the topsoil, extract the thin veins of coal, and leave useless rubble in the wake.

I came to appreciate the power of public policy to reshape the landscape, literally. Working for four years, a group of lawmakers and citizens succeeded in passing a new surface-mined reclamation act in 1971. It required that most mined land to be returned to its original topography. After I left the legislature in 1973, there were further refinements that require topsoil to be set aside from lesser earth materials and be replaced last as a final top layer.

So today in central-western Illinois someone with a sharp eye can drive by strip-mined land and identify it quickly according to the law in force at the time it was reclaimed. "Pre-law" land (land mined before the first, weak reclamation law of 1961) has rows of sharp ridges and peaks where the drag lines dumped the soil; the steep slopes are generally barren. The 1961 law required miners to "strike off" the tops of the ridges and peaks "where adjacent to public highways"—to soften the eyesore!—and where land was to be sown to pasture. Now the land is returned to its original topography, with the "final cuts" of the drag lines often made into clear water impoundments.

With each proposal to increase the reclamation requirements the lobbyists for the mine operators contended the increased cost would drive them out of operation in Illinois. And indeed there is no mining at present in my old district, though the operators still own much land there. Statewide, however, about the same tonnage of coal was mined in Illinois in 1988 as in 1970, though factors such as demand and sulfur content are more important in this regard than are reclamation costs.

I have been away from natural resource issues since the early 1970s, though it is time for all of us in Illinois to refresh and update our understanding. By far the best place to start is with three compilations of articles written for *Illinois Issues* by James Krohe Jr., who writes with impressive thoughtfulness and clarity. They are titled *Water Resources in Illinois* (1982), *Breadbasket or Dustbowl* (1982), and *Toxics and Risk* (1986). I draw heavily from these sources in the discussion that follows.

Only Kansas and Texas have more prime farmland in the U.S. than does Illinois. (Prime farmland is that with high grain crop productivity.) There are 36 million acres of land in Illinois and 31.4 million are used to grow things. Of this crop acreage, two-thirds is judged to be prime. So we produce a lot, ranking first or second in the nation each year in corn and soybean production, which in 1979 came to about 17.5 percent of the nation's corn and 16.5 percent of U.S. soybeans. Illinois ranks second in the nation in value of crops marketed and first in value of crops exported. As a result, two of every five workers in Illinois are linked directly or indirectly to farming, through jobs in food processing, transportation, marketing, banking, chemicals, and implement manufacturing.

But as Jim Krohe points out, "the distance between Eden and the desert" is a mere six inches of topsoil in many parts of Illinois. And we have been eroding that away with reckless abandon. To draw on Krohe again, average topsoil loss in Illinois is about 6.7 tons per acre annually. Spread over an acre, 6.7 tons of soil makes a layer only as thick as a sheet of paper. Seemingly insignificant, except when the losses cumulate year after year. The Illinois Natural History Survey reports that in recent years Illinois farms have lost 1.5 bushels of topsoil for every bushel of corn grown. As Jim Frank of the Illinois Department of Agriculture puts it: "We are mining the soil of our rich prairie lands just as if we were stripping for coal."

The Illinois EPA has estimated that statewide corn yield per acre in 2010 will be 164 bushels per acre if present erosion trends occur versus 185 bushels if "best management practices" are pursued. That would come to about 250 million bushels of lost production annually, based on present land use and farming practices.

I sense that farmers are becoming more conscious of the costs of erosion. As I drive the 25 miles between the Knox College campus and my country home in far western Illinois, I observe each Fall less of the deep moldboard plowing that turns over the surface cover and bares the rich soil to the ravages of winter winds and water runoff. In its place farmers are using "chisel plowing" that leaves much of the protective cover, or they are experimenting with "no till" practices that leave it all. Soil erosion affects us all, because the soil is water-borne to our water supply, carrying with it chemical fertilizers and pesticides. Soil erosion is probably the number one water pollution source, according to a 1985 report of the Conservation Foundation, a Washington, D.C. research group.

There is a lot of water in Illinois. The state is drained by four of the continent's major streams—the Mississippi, Ohio, Wabash, and Illinois. Illinois is also attached, as Krohe puts it, like a calf to a teat, to Lake Michigan, which is part of the largest fresh water system in the world. In addition there are extensive underground water systems. All are replenished by precipitation that ranges from an average of 32 inches per year in the northeastern counties to 46 inches in the extreme south. Most rain originates in the Gulf of Mexico and the subtropical Atlantic, which—Krohe again with a great metaphor—heave great sighs of wet air into the Midwest.

As a result supply exceeds demand overall. Even in the heavily populated northeast counties near Chicago the ratio of potential water supply to demand is roughly six to one, and at the southern tip of Illinois the ratio is 2500 to 1. So rich are we in water that Governor Thompson and others have referred to the Midwest as the OPEC of water. There has been talk of exporting water to the parched Plains States. Krohe points out that we have been exporting water throughout history, in our corn which contains a gallon per bushel and which requires 2500 gallons to bring each bushel to maturity.

In fact it probably makes more sense to bring jobs to our water than vice versa, for several reasons. First, we are consuming more water each year. Water aquifers under Chicago-area suburbs are being emptied three times faster than they are being recharged, and water tables are dropping as a result. Diminished storage capacity in surface reservoirs downstate due to siltation has caused shortages in some communities. And there may be new demands. Synthetic fuels plants—which might one day turn Illinois high sulfur coal into clean-burning liquid fuel— would gulp as much as 81 million gallons per day at each plant. Irrigation of crops has also been increasing significantly in recent years.

Second, the export of water would lower Lake Michigan water levels and create serious problems for navigation and the fishing industry. For example, a lowering the Lake Michigan by one inch could reduce the cargo capacity of certain large ships by 200 tons, and many of these ships make 50 trips across the lake each year.

Other states do covet our water. Groundwater levels are dropping up to six feet a year in the Plains States. It is estimated that within little more than a decade farmers of 15 million acres in the Plains and Southwestern states will have to shift to less water-intensive crops. In its 1985 report on the attractiveness of states as manufacturing locations, the Chicago-based accounting firm of Alexander Grant stated that water shortages cast doubt on future growth for some Sun Belt states, especially Florida, California, and Texas.

The battle for scarce water will grow ever more intense, increasing the net worth of states that have good supplies. But as Coleridge reminded us in *The Rhyme of the Ancient Mariner*, though there may be water everywhere, it doesn't do us much good if it is not fit to drink. Krohe finds that our water quality is probably higher than it was 50 years ago overall. Measured by reductions in the incidence of traditional waterborne disease, which has been the most basic water quality criterion to date, Illinois water earns high marks. As of 1982 there had been only three outbreaks of such disease in the state since 1970.

Though we may have gotten water-borne bacteria under control with the huge investment made in the 1970s in new water treatment plants, we now face the scary, dimly understood challenges posed for our water supply by manmade toxins. We manufacture more than 70,000 chemical substances in the U.S. and we add another thousand to the list each year. Illinois ranks second among the states in the amount of officially-designated hazardous wastes generated each year. Such wastes include heavy metals, solvents, pesticides, and PCBs. Many are suspected carcinogens.

According to Krohe, anywhere from 400 million to 2.7 billion gallons of hazardous wastes are generated in Illinois each year. Nobody really knows, as the range suggests. The wastes are apparently seeping into our drinking water supply. The *New York Times* reported in November 1987 on a farm family in next door Iowa that had been drinking town water because their farm well had been contaminated with pesticides. Then to their consternation the family was told that their nearby town water system and those in 30 other Iowa communities contained trace levels of dissolved pesticides. "What are we to do?" they asked.

Similar findings were reported in Washington County, Illinois in 1988, where minute amounts of Atrazine, Chlordane, and forms of DDT were among the eight pesticides found in both shallow and deep farm wells. The pedologist from the University of Illinois was surprised to find pesticide traces there because Washington County soils are of the claypan type that are difficult to permeate.

I do not write to alarm, and could not do so with authority anyway because I am a social scientist who could not tell Atrazine from Kool-Aid. But farm friends of mine are worried. They are hesitant to talk much about it, because they feel dependent on the chemicals for high production. But after a few beers while watching a Bears game on the tube, several farm neighbors recounted worries to me based on years of working with the undiluted chemicals. They had also heard of studies, such as those cited in the November 22, 1987, *New York Times*, that farmers in Illinois and other Midwestern states have a higher incidence of certain cancers than do other sectors of the population.

I was on Amtrak's Illinois Zephyr in August 1988 sitting in the coffee bar with a farmer, heading from western Illinois toward Chicago across the flat tapestry of corn and soybean fields. At one point the farmer directed my attention to a field that had been "burned" a sickly yellow, apparently by inappropriate application of chemicals, and said, "We're gonna have to get away from that stuff, and quick. It's gettin' into our water." Aware of these growing concerns on the part of its members, the Illinois Farm Bureau weekly newspaper is carrying more stories about how to reduce use of chemicals without reducing yields, through "integrated pest management" practices.

There is urgency to the issue, for as Krohe observes, "Once groundwater supplies are contaminated, they are virtually impossible to reclaim." Underground water aquifers are often miles wide, and toxic pollutants travel slowly through the earth, sometimes taking years to reach a water source.

What do we do about these possible threats? Regulation depends on knowledge, but practically nothing is "known" about the health effects of toxics in the way that it is known that typhoid fever is caused by the Salmonella typhosa bacillus. To date pollution program managers have had the advantage of knowing the relatively few agents of bacterial risk, and they have been able to devise techniques for each. But with thousands of possibly harmful chemical substances, it is like trying to put out a forest fire one tree at a time.

The risk of toxics has proved hard if not impossible to quantify, says Krohe, other than in almost hopelessly wide ranges. For example, the official maximum exposure to formaldehyde allowed under regulations of the U. S. Occupational

Safety and Health Administration is estimated to subject workers to a risk of between 0.7 and 6.2 cancers per 10,000 workers over a 70-year "lifetime" of exposure.

Estimates of risk from exposure to a chemical are expressed separately, that is, in addition to the general risk of contracting cancer that everyone faces. All of us who live to old age share a general risk of about three out of ten of contracting some form of cancer sometime, though this will vary for individuals because of different lifestyles and settings. As a result, former Illinois EPA director Richard Carlson calls official expressions of quantified risk as "totally undecipherable."

So nonexperts like you and me must resort to whatever common sense we can apply in order to define "acceptable risk." This *is* important because matters of science and questions of risk are resolved politically. As political scientist Lynton Caldwell observed 25 years ago, biological facts (about which we generally don't know enough) in conflict with popular truths (that government should protect us, for example) can only be reconciled politically. Conflict not resolvable in the labs will be resolved in the law. Even when the scientists have resolved an issue, public preferences often supercede scientific good sense. For example, Richard Carlson recalls a public hearing at which a lady expressed strong concerns about chemicals in the water supply all the while holding a lighted cigarette in her hand.

Krohe suggests that the model we use for regulating automobile risk might be more sensible for environmental issues than that of trying to quantify an individual's risk for cancer. The public derives such enormous benefits from its use of the auto that we tolerate high social costs in injury, death, and public spending. The risks of both driving and toxics can be reduced but not to zero, and each marginal reduction in risk will likely be more expensive than earlier ones. Auto air bags cost more than seatbelts, for example.

Public attitudes and thus policies toward water have been based on the assumptions that water is abundant, easy to make safe, and a nearly free good, like air. These assumptions are no longer correct. From our vantage point in the Midwest, it is easy to be critical of federal water policies in parts of the West, where the price of water is highly subsidized. For example, according to Terry L. Anderson, farmers in the Central Valley of California pay as little as $5 per-acre-foot for water that costs between $300 and $400 per-acre-foot to deliver.

Experts in Illinois agree, says Krohe, that water is generally priced much too low here as well. Often rates are too low even to cover routine maintenance costs. Thus the real cost of providing dependable water is disguised by deferring needed capital improvements. In effect, elected officials transfer the costs of running their water systems from people voting today to the coming generation. Krohe admonishes us that:

Legislating for scarcity—by charging for what used to be free, by allocating what used to be available to all, by not allowing what used to be automatic—is a skill not yet learned. The question seems not to be whether Illinois will learn it but how soon. Even Illinois cannot continue forever to have its water and drink it too.

If you have ploughed this far in the chapter you can tell I am not the world's foremost authority on the quality of life. But I would be wary of anyone who claims to be. My purpose in this chapter is to remind us that we nonexperts play a large role in determining what that quality of life will be. A few years ago Illinois EPA director Carlson lamented, "Everybody wants someone else to make the decisions and they want decisions that result in absolute safety. But absolute safety is impossible... What degree of chemical safety do people want?"

There we have toxic politics in a nutshell, says Krohe—an anxious public looking to its public protectors for guidance, and instead of getting an easy answer it finds the protectors looking right back through the looking glass.

We need to intensify public discussion of quality-of-life issues. When the environmental movement subsided in the mid-1970s so did public policy debate on the matter. This can be resuscitated in part through the visible statewide strategic thinking teams that I propose in Chapter 10.

Second, we should provide more support and encouragement to the Environmental Consensus Forum that is administered by the University of Illinois School of Public Health. This is a structured setting in which parties representing industry and citizen groups concerned about the environment come together in a nonadversarial setting to determine if consensus can be reached on complicated issues. The Forum was successful in the mid-1980s in developing a compromise proposal to ban landfilling of hazardous wastes; it eventually became law.

Consensus is not always possible nor desirable in shaping public policy. The search for consensus can be an important intellectual and practical tool, however, for exploring options for thorny issues. I participated in the development of this consensus forum and came away convinced that it can increase understanding and reduce differences among legitimate interests.

Most important, we need to develop a clear public ethic about the quality of life we want to achieve. Without this, public officials will lack a compass to guide their decisions. They will continue to look out to the public and be met by rather blank stares. An ethic needs to be articulated and this takes leadership. Otherwise you and I will opt for the load that is lightest at the moment. We will resist paying full cost now for goods that create disposal hazards and health risks later.

Krohe finds that some executives are abandoning the traditional three Ds of corporate pollution policy—Damn, Deny, and Delay—in favor of a new ethic of three Rs—Reduce, Reuse, and Recycle. This simple yet profound change in ethic is one we need to adopt as part of our public ethic, along with the policies of Conserving, Protecting, and Paying a Price that Reflects Full Cost.

A Time for Rural Regrouping

Wyoming, Illinois (pop. 1,600) won a Governor's Hometown Award this summer for its active "betterment association." That same week Wyoming's largest employer announced it was leaving town with its 150 jobs. Also that same week the town's largest retailer, a farm implement dealer, announced he was closing the family business after four decades of operation.

Sometimes you can't win for losin'.

Illinois has about 1,000 small towns, more than any state but Texas. Many of them are really hurting, because of job and population loss. Central-western Illinois, where Wyoming is situated, has lost about 10 percent of its population since 1980!

Bad as things are, we have to keep things in perspective. Rural Illinois has been losing people since the end of the nineteenth century. Farm problems and manufacturing job losses in nearby cities have been especially severe recently, but the trend has been in place a long time. The basic response has been to set up economic development agencies to attract employers via spiffy brochures, tax breaks, and low-cost capital. The problem is that lebenty-seben thousand towns big and small have all been doing the same thing, so the net gain overall is probably close to nil.

Political economist Bill Galston has done a hard-headed analysis of the comparative advantages of urban and rural America. In sum he says that urban areas will continue to have strong advantages overall in education, job skills, and ability to respond to change. Rural settings will have lower costs of labor and housing, and for some—especially the increasing ranks of prosperous retirees—the tranquil rural life may represent better quality.

Rural and small town Illinois do have some strengths that can be developed, but only over the long haul. First, people want to live in small towns. In 1985 the Gallup Survey asked respondents their preferences, "If you could live anywhere you wished..." Half preferred small towns or rural areas; the figure jumped to 60 percent when the category "large town" (10-50,000) was included.

Second, today more people are able to work from where they live, through the use of gizmos called work stations like the one I'm typing this on, from my rural home.

Third, in the future the rich soil of the Midwest will be devoting much of its productivity to industrial purposes, as in fuels, biodegradable paper products, and manufacturing chemicals. L.R. Princen, director of the U.S. Northern Research Laboratory in Peoria, predicts that in a decade up to one quarter of our farmland will be devoted to industrial products.

Fourth, there is still a lot of leadership talent in rural Illinois, especially among young farmers.

I believe the key to rural revival lies in taking steps now that will bear fruit, not next year but in the next decade and beyond. It won't be easy. Since there are fewer of us, we need to regroup around our strengths and the institutions that define us, such as our schools. Here are illustrations.

1. Superior rural schools. A key factor in residential location is the quality of the local schools. Most city folks tend to think of rural schools as short on course offerings and quality. I

INTO THE SUNSET

propose, for example, that rural schools leap ahead of most suburban schools by offering one or more foreign languages continually from early in grammar school through high school. This would take creative leadership and cooperation among schools. It would be expensive, but ought to be done anyway, and if publicized effectively could cause families of executives in nearby cities to take positive notice.

2. Leadership regrouping. Creative leaders, not government programs, will ultimately determine the destinies of rural communities. Main Street leadership has dried up in many towns, as storefronts have been shuttered. The Illinois Farm Bureau, however, has been nurturing leadership skills and confidence among its young men and women through impressive executive training programs.

Unfortunately, the Farm Bureau—by far the strongest rural group in Illinois—has never had much interest in the broader issues of farm town and rural development. I think that is changing, however, as farmers see the quality of their lives affected by weakened market towns and struggling schools. I challenge the Farm Bureau to establish a statewide "rural leaders roundtable," for purposes of creative cooperation, and second, to broaden the mission of the Farm Bureau to include rural issues generally.

3. Establish a "rural caucus" within the Illinois legislature. This group of about one-fifth of all lawmakers could meet regularly to discuss problems of mutual concern. While government cannot solve rural problems, policy change is often necessary to facilitate new approaches. For example, extensive foreign language training in rural schools would probably require waiver of strict teacher certification rules.

4. Preserve the best of the past. Wherever possible, maintain nineteenth century railroad stations and red-brick main street buildings. Historic preservation has been of great value in the revival of many New England towns.

Some small towns will revive; others not. Rural communities that are effective in regrouping to retain and attract creative, enterprising people will have the best opportunities to sustain themselves and even flourish.

Chapter 8

Budgeting and Taxing for a New Game Plan

When I mention budgeting in my public policy course at Knox College, eyes begin to glaze over. My captive students cast furtive glances at the ol' clock on the wall to see how soon until they are saved by the bell. Quickly I point out that budgets are actually fascinating. They are the score cards of politics, as they tally in dollars the winners and losers in the game of who gets what in society.

Budgets reflect the allocation of our values. The importance or value we attach to student financial aid is reflected in the amount we appropriate in the budget for that purpose. Each object of our spending is in intense competition with all others, because the dollars available are always in scarce supply relative to the demand for them. Aid for college students is in competition not only with spending for prisons and county fairs, but also with programs for mentally retarded adults and poor children, though we resist thinking about it in those terms.

In the Illinois legislature I served on the House Appropriations Committee. This is where values are formally allocated, where votes are taken each year on several hundred bills that propose to spend state monies. Here I learned lessons central to politics. First, everyone who came before us favored spending. Rarely did anyone testify in opposition to spending. Retired teachers wanted higher pension benefits; artists wanted more grants to local arts groups; farmers wanted improvements at county fair grounds; people with kidney dysfunction wanted the state to buy more dialysis machines.

Second, almost every purpose appeared to have some merit.

Third, the budget of a big state is incomprehensible to all but a handful of career specialists. For Fiscal Year 1989 (which began July 1, 1988), Governor Thompson presented a budget to the legislature of three hefty volumes that ran to 1,150 pages of fine print. A lawmaker who tries to read the whole of it is a masochist immediately eligible for admittance to one of our mental health facilities.

Fourth, there is a strong pull to go about budgeting in an incremental fashion. That is, lawmakers start with what was spent last year, assuming that it was basically sensible, and then they focus scrutiny on how much of an increase, or increment, is proposed for the coming year. Public management specialists like me criticize this as inadequate, but I found myself relying on the same approach in the legislature, in part because there is so little time to examine closely each of about 500 appropriations bills. In the early 1960s, political scientist Thomas J. Anton found that in one session the House Appropriations Committee spent an average of only three minutes in public hearings on each bill!

Fifth, because the state budget is unfathomable, candidates for office can get away with promises that they are going to continue all good programs, add some new ones, and do it all for less—simply by cutting the fat and waste out of government! It sells every time.

There is some waste in government, but not much of the old-style waste in which politicians syphoned tax money off to nongovernmental functions. I had an uncle who was both a housepainter and a Republican county chairman in the 1940s. As a reward for his faithful work for the party, he was offered a "ghost payroller" job, for which he would be paid but for which he was not expected to show up to do any work. That is good old-fashioned waste. To uncle's credit, he turned it down, or so my parents told me.

Three decades ago the state auditor was caught having syphoned off more than $1 million to sustain an elegant life style. It was easy for him to do, for awhile anyway, as he was responsible both for issuing the checks and for auditing whether the checks had been issued for an appropriate purpose. He thought they had.

Flagrant waste is kept to a minimum today because of tight oversight of spending provided by the compliance and performance audits of the Auditor General, a constitutional officer of the legislative branch. In addition, the offices of state Comptroller and Treasurer conduct separate pre- and post-audits of state spending. As a result, the amount of money wasted through corrupt or ill-advised spending is a minute fraction of the total budget, certainly not enough to accomplish the legerdemain of candidates who promise to do much more with less.

In this chapter I present a budget sketch that explains what my major proposals would cost you, and how I think we ought to pay the bills. In response to fervent pleas from my publisher, I spare you much detail. If you had not yet guessed, I should forewarn you that I propose that Illinois invest significantly more in order to meet fundamental responsibilities and challenges.

Background on State Spending and Taxing

We have been asking state government to do ever more in recent years. When I entered the state legislature in 1969 the medical care program for the indigent (Medicaid) was new and cost little. Today it takes $2 billion of the state budget. In 1988 the legislature voted a new program to help those who can no longer get health insurance, but voted against funding it, for lack of money. Later in the year the lawmakers voted to fund it, but the governor vetoed the spending, citing lack of money. Does anyone seriously expect health care costs to do other than increase in the future, given the longer lives we lead and the ever more exotic health technologies we all insist on using?

In his fiscal year 1989 budget, Governor Thompson listed 21 new program initiatives adopted either by the legislature or by administrative action of the governor since 1985. Here are a few of them: education reforms; expanded probation services; expanded circuit breaker (property tax) relief for the elderly; missing children searches; AIDS research and education, and asbestos removal in schools. Each of them sounds as if it has some merit, and each was undoubtedly advocated vigorously before the appropriations committees by citizen support groups.

What programs are we terminating to make way for these? None that I can think of, though we did abolish the Spanish-American War Veterans Commission a few years ago, after the last veteran died, as I recall.

Illinois is also going through demographic change that has budget consequences. As I pointed out in Chapter 1, there has been a severe net out-migration of whites in the past decade and increases in the proportion of us who are from minority groups. For reasons of past discrimination and inadequate education, persons from minority groups tend overall to need more of the services that state government provides—education, health, and social welfare—than do whites. So demand for services has been increasing faster than our economy has been growing.

In addition, we have asked the state to get tougher on criminals, which is expensive. Our prisons held about 5,000 inmates in 1969; now we house more than 20,000. To meet these varied increased demands, Illinois spent $500 million more in fiscal years 1986 and 1987 than we took in. By 1988 the state was slowing our tax refunds as well as payments to hospitals and nursing homes, for lack of money.

Governor Thompson sought tax increases in both 1987 and 1988, without success. There were many factors at play. Simply put, many lawmakers were not strongly persuaded that a tax hike would make enough of a difference in the outcomes of our education and social service systems to justify the political pain of voting for a tax increase.

An annual budget of $18-22 billion for fiscal year 1989 is basically incomprehensible ($18+ billion in actual revenues; $22+ billion in total appropriations, some of which won't be spent during the fiscal year). Thus many lawmakers conclude that somehow money can be found within that awesome amount to do whatever new things need to be done. But it cannot be found, apparently not in the amounts needed to provide early education services to all poor children at risk of failure. The state school board asked for enough money to provide these services to 18,500 of the state's 112,000 three- and four-year-olds at risk (up from 6,900 served in fiscal 1988), but it received enough to serve a total of only 11,000, according to the Illinois State Board of Education.

What is the revenue situation in Illinois? The accompanying pie chart at Figure 8.1 shows that the state income tax is our biggest revenue source, followed by the federal government, and then the five percent state sales tax. I voted for the income tax when it was enacted in 1969 (and I was re-elected without

Figure 8.1. Estimated Illinois revenues by source, for all appropriated funds, fiscal year 1989.

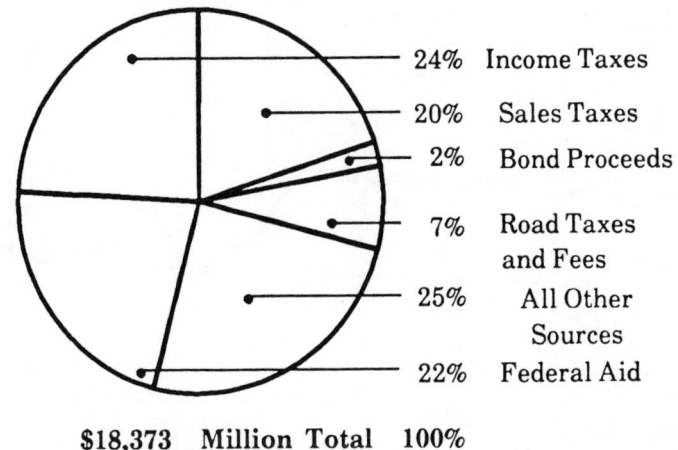

- 24% Income Taxes
- 20% Sales Taxes
- 2% Bond Proceeds
- 7% Road Taxes and Fees
- 25% All Other Sources
- 22% Federal Aid

$18,373 Million Total 100%

Source: *Illinois State Budget, Fiscal Year 1989.* Office of the Governor, Springfield, 1988.

---

opposition a year later, so it did not sound my political death knell). The rate was set at 2.5 percent for individuals and 4.0 percent for corporations; the rate is the same 20 years later. In the meantime, a number of taxes have gone up and down.

In 1985 the Illinois Economic and Fiscal Commission (IEFC) identified 42 changes that had reduced state tax revenues by $835 million per year from what would have been generated otherwise. Examples include the deduction of residential property taxes from state income tax liability, as well as 12 exemptions from the sales tax for the purchase of products such as ethanol and graphic arts equipment.

At the same time there have been certain increases, as in the rate of the state sales tax from four to five percent. On balance, state tax burden per $1,000 of income is less than it was in 1971, as Figure 8.2 illustrates.

Federal funds declined as a part of our state budget during the Reagan presidency, from about 25 percent of the Illinois budget in 1981 to 22 percent in 1989. Because of continuing

Figure 8.2. The Illinois tax burden. State tax sources as percentage of Illinois personal income.

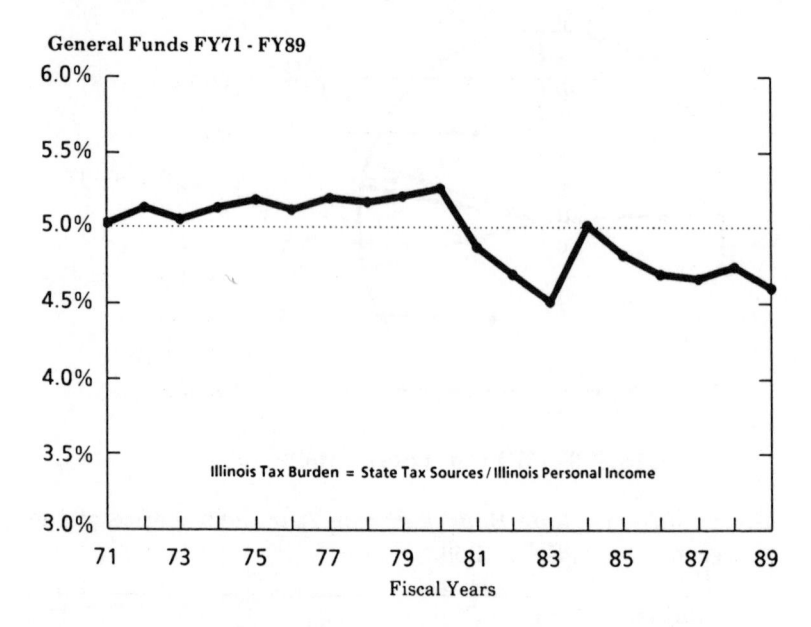

General Funds FY71 - FY89

Illinois Tax Burden = State Tax Sources / Illinois Personal Income

Fiscal Years

Source: *Illinois State Budget, Fiscal Year 1989.* Office of the Governor, Springfield, 1988.

---

federal government deficits, federal funds for Illinois are not expected to increase significantly, and may continue to slide as a percentage of the total state budget.

Each year total state revenues grow somewhat, in large part because of inflation. This is called "natural growth." For fiscal 1989 this will amount to about $500 million, which is a lot of money, but only about four percent of fiscal 1988 revenues from state sources, a smaller percentage than the rate of inflation. Many lawmakers see that extra $500 million and say, "That's where we'll get the money for new programs," without computing that inflation will increase the cost of goods, services, and salaries that state government has to purchase.

During the 1970s natural growth in revenues did occur at rates greater than those for inflation. In the 1980s, however, this natural growth tended to lag behind the rate of inflation. Writing in the June 1988 *Illinois Business Review*, deputy state budget director Richard Kolhauser identifies several reasons for the change. Our economy was robust in the 1970s and federal funds were flowing to the states. Utility tax revenue went up rapidly as it was pegged to energy prices, which skyrocketed. The new lottery was a new revenue source for the state that grew rapidly in the late 1970s and early 1980s.

In recent years there has been a shift from high-paid manufacturing jobs to lower-paid service sector jobs, slowing growth in income tax revenues. The flow of federal funds has slowed. Utility taxes have been capped. Lottery revenue growth has ended, and has begun to decline. (That is why the advertising pitches became more shrill in 1988.) There has been an increase in service sector activity, but services are not taxed in Illinois.

Kolhauser was pessimistic in 1988 about chances for a return soon to natural growth in state revenues that would keep pace with the economy. Since then, however, the Illinois economy has been expanding more rapidly than had been predicted, and revenue growth appears to have been keeping pace with inflation. The point remains that "natural growth" in state government revenue has been accompanied by comparable or even greater increases in the natural costs of doing state business, and so this additional revenue is not readily available for new or expanded programs.

Illinois—High Tax or Low Tax State?

Is Illinois a high tax state? It depends—on whether you evaluate our taxes on the basis of taxation per person or per $1,000 of personal income, and on whether you include local taxes in the mix. If you want to make the case that Illinois has a high tax burden you show that total state *and* local taxes in Illinois of $1,546 *per person* for fiscal year 1986 placed our state 17th highest among the 50 states. If you want to argue the opposite you point out that *state* tax collections of $57.65 *per $1,000 of personal income* rank us low, 41st out of 50 states.

These different rankings come about basically because: 1) Illinois has more income per capita than most states, and 2) we rely more heavily on local taxes than most states and less so on the state income tax. (See Figure 8.3.) The U.S. Advisory

Commission on Intergovernmental Relations says that Illinois makes more state and local tax effort than the average state. This conclusion is based on complicated assumptions about a nationally uniform set of tax bases and tax rates.

On the other hand, Thomas Mortenson, a senior analyst with the American College Testing Program, wrote in 1984 that, "If the people of Illinois taxed themselves at the average tax effort for all states in fiscal year 1982, they would share roughly $2.8 billion more of their personal income with state and local governments." He was using the personal income measure rather than per capita basis for his analysis.

Rather than get beyond my intellectual depth on this topic, let me observe that most Illinois residents think their taxes are too high now. However, there is capacity to tax more, even significantly more according to Mortenson, *if* we feel it important to do so.

Would higher taxes hurt or help the state economy overall? Here again, you take your side and you pick your arguments. In 1988 Lester Brann, the feisty president of the Illinois State

Chamber of Commerce, traveled the state with the message that a tax increase would retard economic growth and development. He had a sheaf of figures in hand to buttress his case. On the other hand, John Hogan, business college dean at the University of Illinois in Urbana, cited a ten-year study of the relative effects of education and taxes. Reported in the *Illinois Business Review*, the study concluded that the positive effect of education outweighed the negative effect of a tax increase by a factor of more than two to one.

Figure 8.3. Tax capacity and tax revenue in Illinois in 1985 compared with average U.S. capacity.* (Illinois is represented by the black column.)

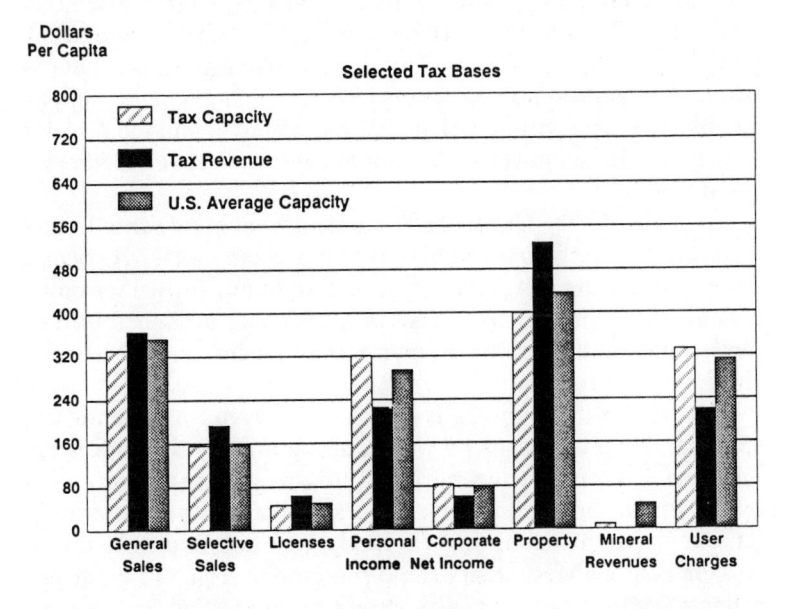

Source: *Measuring State Fiscal Capacity, 1987 Edition.* U.S. Advisory Commission on Intergovernmental Relations, Washington, D.C., December 1987.

* Tax capacity is defined here as the dollar amount of revenue that each state would raise if it applied a nationally uniform set of tax rates to a common set of tax bases.

Beyond the Margins of Our Mediocrity

There will be an increase in general state taxes sometime in the next few years simply because our revenue base is not adequate to fulfill our aspirations, nor even to meet our expectations. Whether our tax burden is heavy or modest, it has been declining while at the same time service needs for a changing population have been increasing. If an increase does not come sooner, it will be triggered some day by prison riots at Joliet or Pontiac or by visuals on the evening news of nursing home patients thrown out on the street because of unpaid state bills.

Most Illinois residents want to be proud of their state; that is human nature. We want excellent schools and universities and a respected, productive workforce. The reality is that Illinois has become a state that can best be characterized as mediocre, that is, as the dictionary defines it, "of moderate to low quality; average." Illinois—The Barely Average State. That is what we are nationally in terms of school achievement, college completion rates, preparation of our workforce, and most social indicators. In comparison with Japan, we are not even mediocre, we are poor.

In June of 1988 Governor Thompson went before the Illinois General Assembly to plead his case for a tax increase. He began eloquently, as he can: "By not investing in our future we pay a human toll today in lives lost to ignorance, broken families, lawlessness and drug addiction, unemployment.... If we lose the child, we lose the adult."

He went on to list literally scores of programs in need and the specific dollar increases he would provide them through a tax increase. The speech degenerated into a mish-mash that tended to confirm the lawmakers' worst fears—a little bit here and there for every program, and we'll likely not see a difference in outcomes anywhere, or so I could imagine several of my former colleagues thinking. The tax increase proposal died three weeks later without even coming to a vote in either house of the legislature.

Nowhere did he call for going beyond the margins of our mediocrity. There was no pledge that together we achieve challenging goals that would match our loftiest aspirations. There was no commitment that every child at-risk be given a good shot at getting to the same starting line for formal education that children from the good neighborhoods start from. There was no pledge that our education system once again become among the best in the world.

In his speech the governor called for a "modest tax increase" that would have increased total state revenues about six percent. You and I can argue about whether this proposal to increase the state income tax rate on individuals from 2.5 percent to 3.5 percent is modest or major. Whichever, it would not move Illinois beyond the margins of mediocrity because it would not represent the investment needed to achieve the fundamental goals I set out in the preceding paragraph.

So in addition to the governor's litany of unmet needs and adopted but unfunded new policy initiatives in mental health, public health, and children's services, to which I subscribe, there must be certain fundamental additional investments if we are to move beyond mediocrity.

First, we need to make the commitment that all poor children at risk will get the support that a tiny fraction now get. Based on estimates of $2,000 per child per year and about 200,000 children ages 2-4 at risk, I estimate unmet need of $400 million per year. Clearly that could not all be invested wisely in the first year, as we are not organized to provide that much additional help immediately. Nevertheless we need to make the commitment now and anticipate the cost.

Second, we have to lengthen the school calendar from 176 to about 210 classroom days per year. The Japanese calendar is 240 days, though that includes half-days on Saturday; many European school calendars are more than 200 days in length. I acknowledge that learning and number of days taught cannot be correlated perfectly. Over recent decades, however, we have made the opposite, even less defensible assumption—that more and more subjects can be learned in the same amount of time as before. We have been squeezing more and more curricular mandates—from consumer ed to conservation ed to drug abuse ed to drivers ed—into the same limited school day and school year.

If we want to compete with Japan in math and science and with Europeans in foreign languages, then we simply have to devote more time to learning, inside the classroom and in homework.

I estimate that we now spend a total of $7 billion per year in Illinois in state and local revenues on education, from kindergarten through senior high school. I extrapolate that it would cost an additional $1 billion to extend the school year by 30 days. I propose that all this additional investment be paid from state taxes, none from local property taxes. By the way, I estimate this fundamental change in the way we would go about educating our young people would increase teacher salaries 15-20 percent, addressing another problem in education.

To those who respond that it cannot be done, I respond simply that it is being done elsewhere, with apparently salutary results. If we cannot make a similar commitment, it represents a lack of will and discipline that will consign our children to a mediocre future, or worse, in a tough, competitive world.

Investing to Get Beyond Our Mediocrity

I estimate that approximately $2.5 billion in annual new revenue would be required to fund my proposals for fundamental change and to meet the general budget increase proposed by Governor Thompson in the Spring of 1988. That would represent a significant 13 percent increase in total state spending. It would still be less, however, than the $2.8 billion that policy analyst Mortenson said in 1982 would be required to bring Illinois up to the national average in tax effort, based on personal income.

By any measure this is more than modest I grant you, yet I am proposing more than modest change.

There are at least a couple of ways this new revenue could be raised. Public finance specialists often recommend that we tax consumption of the services provided by repairmen, cleaners, lawyers, hair stylists, and others. Services are not taxed in Illinois; a few states, such as Iowa, tax a broad range of them. John Mikesell, a leading student of taxation, writes:

> There is no reason why private purchases of services should be treated differently from purchases of tangible personal property. Both are consumption expenditures; to tax commodity purchases but not service purchases discriminates according to consumption preferences and sacrifices a portion of the legitimate tax base.

BUDGETING AND TAXING 123

"AW, THAT'S NOT A GHOST—THAT'S SOMEONE OPENING THEIR PROPERTY TAX BILL."

Governor Thompson hoisted this idea up the flag pole in 1987 where it was shot down quickly by the heavy artillery from the interest groups representing service providers. About the same time, Florida lawmakers repealed the service tax they had adopted a few months earlier, unable to withstand the barrage of public outrage. Just because professors like me think a tax makes sense does not mean the public will buy it.

Surveys show consistently the public finds the income tax less offensive than the sales tax and much less odious than the property tax. The problem in Illinois is, as I see it anyway, that the state constitution requires a flat-rate income tax in which all income, whether $10,000 or $200,000, must be taxed at the same rate. Many economists consider this regressive, that is, unfair to the poor because the tax is unrelated to a person's ability to pay.

In addition to the flat-rate income tax, Illinois relies more heavily on the local property tax than do most states, as shown in Figure 8.3. This levy is also generally unrelated to ability to pay or to public services received, as farmers will attest. According to Voices for Illinois Children, a child advocacy group, the poorest 20 percent of taxpayers in Illinois pay 9.6 percent of their incomes in state and local taxes while the richest one percent pay 4.3 percent of their incomes in those taxes.

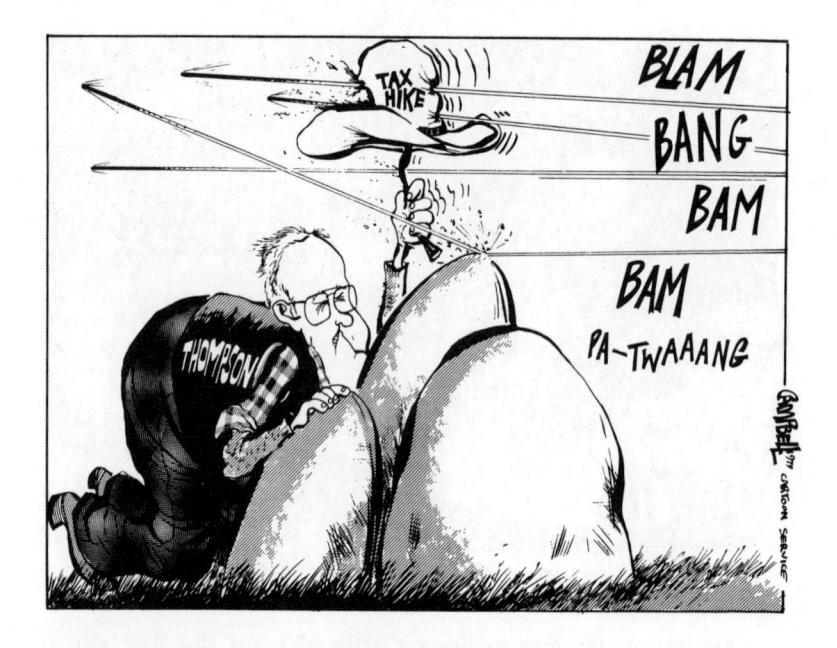

The state income tax in Illinois can be made somewhat less regressive by increasing the standard individual exemption that each of us subtracts from our taxable income. The standard exemption in Illinois is the same $1,000 per person established in 1969. Since then inflation has eroded the value of that exemption by more than half. As a result, a family of four with an annual earned income of $10,000, which is below the national poverty line, pays an Illinois income tax of $150.

Proposals for Tax Increases and Changes

Throughout this book I have sought to persuade that we must make fundamental changes in our commitments to one another if we want our state and our children to be able to compete. I find the following conclusion inescapable—we cannot make the new commitments and achieve lofty goals with more tax money alone, nor can we achieve them without more money, significantly more money.

I propose that we raise the income tax rate on individuals

BUDGETING AND TAXING   125

Figure 8.4. Tax consequences of changes in the individual income tax as proposed by author in this chapter.

taxable income	family size	1988 rate of 2.5% $1,000 exemption	proposed 5.0% rate $2,500 exemption	tax difference
$10,000	4	$ 150	$ 0	- 150
10,000	2	200	250	+ 50
20,000	4	400	500	+ 100
20,000	2	450	750	+ 300
50,000	4	1150	2000	+ 850
50,000	2	1200	2250	+1050

from 2.5 percent to 5.0 percent. I propose that we increase the standard exemption to $2,500 per person. This would shield from taxation more income of poor families with children.

Proposals to increase the individual tax rate generally include proportionate increases for the corporate income tax, which would take it from 4.0 to 8.0 percent. I recommend we raise the corporate rate only to the same 5.0 percent as for individuals. This would help maintain a business climate that has improved in recent years. This tax generates less money than many imagine and is passed on to consumers for the mostpart anyway. In fact, the state lottery has been raising almost as much net revenue as the tax on corporate income.

These increases and changes would generate about $2.5 billion in net additional annual revenues. Because of the change in the standard exemption, a few taxpayers would pay less; many would pay a little to somewhat more. More prosperous taxpayers, especially single ones like me, would face a hefty increase. Figure 8.4 displays the tax consequences for several families of different incomes and family size. The state does not tax pension income so that part of senior citizen income would not be affected.

Several states have higher income tax rates than I propose, though that alone certainly does not justify the major increase I propose here. Two states—Nevada and New Hampshire—do not even have an income tax. My proposals are not driven by tax rates elsewhere, however. They are driven by a determination of the resources needed to accomplish specific goals for children and education. We can afford the proposals, but not without some sacrifice.

Chapter 9

Managing the State

Illinois state government is big business. It is not run like a business, however, nor can it be. There are no profit-and-loss measures of accountability in state government. Indeed, state agencies feel a strong need to spend all their money by the end of the fiscal year, rather than to save funds; otherwise their budgets might be cut the next year. On-the-job performance is also difficult to assess. The quality of foster care provided an abused child is more difficult to evaluate than is the production rate of zero-defect garden tractors.

The lack of a clear bottom line in government allows a governor and his agency managers to slip into fuzzy measures of management success. As acting director of state agencies on three occasions, I found "no news is good news" to be a leading measure of how well you were doing. That is, if you could keep bad news about your agency from popping up in the newspapers, then presumably you were doing all right. Others measures of success: prevent problems from reaching the governor's desk, avoid public criticism, stay within your budget, and "keep the lid on" situations that could become volatile, as in prisons.

I do not want to downplay the importance of these measures. If you are operating with significantly less money than you need to satisfy the expectations of the media and public, then meeting these measures can represent signal accomplishment. Unfortunately, fuzzy measures of accountability fail to provide either the chief executive or the public a clear sense of how well or poorly services are being delivered.

The chief executive of a major corporation has more independent authority to take decisive action than does the chief executive of Illinois. For instance, in 1988 Lee Iaccoca of

Chrysler closed a major production facility in Kenosha, Wisconsin on a moment's notice, and there was not much anybody could do about it. General Motors also announced plans in 1988 to close a dozen of its older production plants. There will be resistance from unions and civic leaders, but the plants will be closed.

Should a governor even hint at closing an under-utilized public university, there would be hell to pay, from local legislators, party leaders, media, the chamber of commerce, students, alums, and citizens. The governor would not even have the direct authority to do so anyway, for the jurisdiction lies with an independent board and in state statute.

It is true that Illinois governors were able to close seven outdated mental health "hospitals" and "schools" over the past 20 years. Other good candidates for closure were not shuttered, because of successful political opposition. Even where facilities were closed, as in Lincoln and Galesburg, they were replaced in part at least with other state facilities (new prisons).

Management of state government is shared. A governor operates within a web of legitimate interests. For most interest groups, management efficiency and effectiveness are less important than are increased state funding and bureaucratic responsiveness to interest group concerns. For a description of this web and of management in Illinois state government generally, see a book I put together, *Inside State Government: A Primer for Illinois Managers*, cited in the bibliography.

Though not a business, state government can become more productive, responsive, and accountable to its citizens. In this chapter I attempt to show how.

Reorganize the Governor's Office, Not the Agencies

If tradition is a guide, candidates for governor in 1990 will make clarion calls for the streamlining of state government, ostensibly for purposes of efficiency and economy and to cut "the bloated bureaucracy." This theme carried Frank Lowden into the Illinois governorship in 1916 and almost to the presidency four years later. He implemented recommendations of a "Commission on Economy and Efficiency" by consolidating more than 100 boards and commissions into nine departments.

With more than 60 agencies on the organization chart linked

directly to the governor, Illinois appears once again to be a good candidate for major consolidation. No executive can directly manage that "span of control," and the governor doesn't. In a year's time the governor will not meet once with many agency heads, unless there are major problems. He has a staff of about 200, including those in the Bureau of the Budget, who serve as links between him and the agencies.

The agencies are organized into functionally related "subcabinets" for human services, natural resources, economic development, and management. (See Table 9.1 for the groupings of major agencies within the subcabinets.) The subcabinets don't often arrive at major policy decisions, but they do serve the purpose, as one director put it, "of bringing us together to talk to each other on a regular basis. It is incredible to me how little directors see of one another."

Table 9.1. Subcabinets of the Executive Office of the Governor, 1982.

Natural Resources
Department of Agriculture
Department of Conservation
Environmental Protection Agency
Emergency Services and Disaster Agency
Department of Energy and Natural Resources
Department of Mines and Minerals
Department of Nuclear Safety
Illinois Department of Transportation
— Division of Water Resources

Human Services
Department on Aging
Department of Children and Family Services
Department of Mental Health and Developmental Disabilities
Department of Public Aid
Department of Public Health
Department of Rehabilitation Services

Economic Development
Department of Commerce and Community Affairs
Environmental Protection Agency
Housing Development Authority
Industrial Development Authority
Industrial Commission
Department of Insurance
Department of Labor
Department of Revenue
Department of Transportation

Management
Capital Development Board
Department of Central Management Services
Department of Human Rights

Source: James D. Nowlan, ed., *Inside State Government: A Primer for Illinois Managers*, Institute of Government and Public Affairs, University of Illinois, 1983.

The governor's office presents a labyrinth for an agency director. There are the deputy governor, a separate chief of staff, and their assistants. There is a "program staff" of more than 20 professionals, each assigned to be the liaison between the governor's office and one or more agencies. The Bureau of the Budget also assigns a young analyst to oversee an agency's budget, and the analyst has a division chief who is interested in the agency. Then there are staffers from the governor's legal, legislative, patronage, and press offices. All of these people want to tell the agency director how to do his or her job. But with the exception of the deputy governor, they lack authority to give a director the "go ahead" on a course of action when the agency director feels he needs it.

A new governor would also find reorganization an attractive tool because it would assist him in "grabbing the reins" of power by shaking up an entrenched bureaucracy. Organizational arrangements are not neutral; organization is one way of expressing commitment, influencing program direction, and ordering priorities. For example, were a governor foolish enough to try to fold the Department of Agriculture into a Department of Conservation, Natural Resources, *and* Agriculture, he would be signaling a diminished importance for the aggies. Such a governor would find that reorganization of agencies can also be extremely costly—in time, effort, political credits, and opportunity costs—because of the opposition that would be aroused among interest groups, bureaucrats, and legislative patrons of agencies like agriculture.

The standard response to the fragmentation represented by 60 agencies that supposedly report directly to the chief executive is to consolidate them into a few "super agencies" such as those represented by the titles of the subcabinets in Table 9.1.

I do not think that would change anything fundamentally, as the 60 former agencies would be transformed into about the same number of "divisions" or "bureaus" under the super agency heads. The immense effort required to reorganize—with only fair to decent chance of significant success—would divert a new chief executive from more fundamental policy pursuits.

Agency heads *would* be able to operate more effectively if they could get clearer, quicker guidance from the governor's office (though several strong agency heads have taken advantage of the ambiguity to proceed decisively in the absence of clear direction). There also needs to be closer coordination and cooperation among agencies with related functions.

These problems can be addressed by reorganizing the governor's office rather than the agencies. I propose that in place of the 20 program staff liaison to the agencies—who are quite capable but almost invisible—that we create four strong, visible, politically-experienced "special assistants," one for each of the subcabinets. These special assistants—another title might be "secretary to the cabinet"—would work directly with the governor and his deputy and would serve as convenors of regular meetings of the subcabinets, at which they could speak with the clear authority of the governor.

This could clarify lines of communications in both directions. It could also divide responsibilities more appropriately, with the special assistants responsible primarily for policy development and political considerations, while the agency heads could be buffered a bit more from political matters and have increased time for agency management.

Reduce Patronage Pressures

Abolition, or at least reform, of political patronage is another popular cry of gubernatorial aspirants. The last three successful candidates—Ogilvie, Walker, and Thompson—all called for patronage reform. In office, however, each used this tool for dispensing jobs with increasing intensity through his years in office.

Political patronage is the term for awarding governmental jobs to persons who are sponsored by "patrons" such as county political party leaders, state legislators, or the elected official who controls the positions. When I was a child I recall that our neighbor, Jack Benedict, a Republican, lost his position as a state policeman after Democrat Adlai Stevenson was elected governor in 1948. Patronage was the political way of life then, part of the political culture. Benedict went back to work at a gasoline station; he understood that "to the victor belongs the spoils."

Stevenson took the state police out of politics in 1949. The big change in personnel practices came in 1972, however, when a federal court in Chicago decreed that firing of governmental employes because of political affiliation denied equal protection under the laws. Thus, since the governor's office can no longer fire employes on a wholesale basis to make room for its own candidates, the governor's patronage assistants focus on job vacancies as they arise.

Prospective employees are required first to show their merit by meeting minimum education levels and through written and oral examinations. For most job openings, more than one candidate scores an "A" or top grade. The governor's office may select any candidate on the "A roster." The patronage staff attempts to get job applicants with political patrons qualified by examination, so they can then be selected. (This is a simplified explanation of a complex personnel hiring process; for more detail, see the chapter on this topic in *Inside State Government*.)

Under Thompson the influence of patronage has become progressively stronger until almost every opening—even for temporary clerks and student summer internships—is scrutinized closely to see if any patron has a candidate for the opening.

Patronage used to be awarded most often to satisfy political party organizations. At present the governor's office also uses patronage as a tool in working with state legislators of both parties. For example, at the opening of each legislative session one powerful Democratic state senator takes a long list of patronage demands to the Republican governor's office. The implicit trade is that if the job requests are fulfilled, this senate committee chairman will look more kindly on pieces of the governor's legislative program that come before him.

That is a political benefit. There are also costs. Job vacancies have been held open for six months and longer while the governor's patronage office sought to find or qualify candidates for the slots. This hinders agency management and lowers morale of agency staff who perceive the governor's office is more concerned with political considerations than with professional management of the agencies.

The social culture of Illinois considers patronage a standard operating procedure. You are supposed to help your own get jobs if you can, in government if need be. This culture stands in marked contrast to that in neighboring Wisconsin where old-fashioned patronage is anathema. If a new governor of Illinois tried to terminate patronage cold turkey, the withdrawal pains would engender screams of reaction from the legislature that would sour working relationships seriously for several years. This would seriously weaken a governor's capacity to generate fundamental policy change.

Many legislators know that patronage abuse affects the administration of government. A governor who set clear, understandable limits on patronage upon entering office—and stuck to them—could generate acceptance for the guidelines, and even appreciation from many legislators and party leaders who would just as soon rather not be in the personnel business. These limitations could exempt a wide range of mid-level administrative and technical positions from patronage and require that positions not be held open for more than a month solely because of patronage considerations.

The details are less important than are firm steps to establish clear guidelines and eliminate abuses that diminish administrative effectiveness and morale. Then a governor would have to stick to the guidelines. While certain legislators and party officials would push him, just as they are being pushed by job seekers, ultimately they would relent, many of them with a sigh of relief.

Toward a More Professional Bureaucracy

For *Inside State Government*, I surveyed state agency directors who worked for Democratic governor Dan Walker (1973-76) and Republican James Thompson (1977-present). Many of the respondents also had prior management experience in the private sector, so I asked those with business experience how they compared their employes in the governmental and private sectors. Generally they found employes in government to be as capable and motivated overall as those in the business world. Several agency heads observed, however, that their government subordinates were less confident of themselves than were their counterparts in the private sector. In my three tours of duty as an acting agency head I came away impressed with Illinois bureaucrats, yet I sensed they had less *esprit d'corps* and self-respect than was commensurate with their effectiveness.

There may be at least two factors at work here. First is the political culture, mentioned above, that elevates politics and attendantly depreciates administrative professionalism. Second, state government managers have not developed the professional pride that exists in the fraternity of city management, where required graduate-and-continuing education and impressive international networking and information sharing have generated a high level of professionalism. Here are several illustrations of activities that I feel would enhance the professionalism of state government executives.

1. State government management exchanges. To increase cross-fertilization of ideas and management techniques, I recommend that the National Governors' Association implement a program in which senior-level bureaucrats change places with counterparts in other states for periods of several months. For example, the deputy director for operations of the Department of Public Aid might change desks with his or her equal number in California. Additional purposes would be to get fresh evaluations of our state agencies from the visiting managers, and to recharge the batteries of senior managers with the change of milieu.

2. The "state management draft." States do not generally have a good system for attracting the best and the brightest of our nation's graduate students, who are often unaware of the challenges and personal satisfactions that can come from the direct delivery of services to people in need. Why not a national "draft system," akin to the pro football draft. This would entail a major publicity program directed at graduate programs in business, public administration, law, and the sciences.

Each state would present job descriptions for the most challenging junior management posts it was seeking to fill. The challenges that would face "draftees" would have to be a critical selling point, as salaries would not be. Money is not always necessary, fortunately. Under the late governor Richard B. Ogilvie (1969-72) there was a sense of excitement and purpose that attracted White House Fellows and Rhodes Scholars to his staff.

3. Executive training. Illinois has been deficient here. There is no systematic program for executive management training and development. Such would keep managers abreast of changing tools and techniques. More important, it would over time elevate the professionalism of this corps of managers who run a $20 billion service-to-people business.

4. Require graduate degrees for applicants to key professional recruitment programs such as the Legislative Staff Internship Program and the Governor's James Dunn Fellow Program. Along with the Bureau of the Budget (BOB), which recruits nationally for budget analysts, these programs are the leading recruiters of future state government executives.

The legislative staff program originally required master's or law degrees, but does no longer; it ought to. My objectives here are practical, not elitist. Persons with graduate degrees tend to bring with them higher levels of the skills needed in government: clear writing, the capacity to analyze (that is, to break problems into basic elements, assess relationships, and evaluate possible new configurations), and a deeper understanding of public issues. These people are more valuable overall than less well-trained staffers. In addition, they are also more likely to build careers in state government than are the best of those who hold only undergraduate degrees, as the latter often develop a need to leave state government to pursue their own graduate or law degrees.

Managing with an Eye on Outcomes

There *is* a bottom line in government. The media often ask the key measurement questions of agencies: whom do you serve; what are their problems; what do you do for them; how much does it cost, and what are the results? They can get fairly adequate answers to all the questions but the last one—what are the results?

The leading student of results or outcomes monitoring is Reginald Carter, who for eight years was director of evaluation for the Michigan Department of Social Services. He characterizes the problem by saying, "Everybody cares but nobody knows." That is, we sincerely want to help people, but we do not follow those served by state government to find what happened to them afterward. As a result, we don't know much about whether our expensive programs work well or not.

There are several reasons governments rarely monitor outcomes. First, some managers don't want to know the outcomes. Not necessarily because they think they are doing their work badly, but because the public may have unrealistic, unachievable expectations. Job training programs—even very good ones—are not going to place all, or even half, their "clients" in good, permanent jobs. From what we know, 10-20 percent might be a good net placement rate, says Carter.

Second, managers are generally short of staff to do the day-to-day work with their active clients as effectively as they would like, let alone do systematic checks on the progress of former clients. Third, it is thought to be expensive work, especially if the money has to come out of existing agency budgets.

Business evaluates its performance continually, to measure cost effectiveness and return on investment, and to build investor confidence. Indeed, there would be no confidence in a business without precise measures. *Forbes* draws on four profitability measures (return on equity, debt to equity ratio, return on capital, and net profit margin) and two growth measures (sales and earnings per share). These indicators are generally accepted by the private sector, are widely publicized, and are used for comparative purposes. In addition, says Carter, expectation levels for any given year tend to be modest, and the private sector "is only convinced of long term potential after it observes success over at least a five-year period."

In Illinois we spend more than $10 billion a year on direct people services. While we know how much we spent last year on how many citizens, we have almost no idea how much permanent good, if any, we may have done. We do have a relatively new School Report Card that is providing district-by-district aggregate outcomes for graduation rates and pupil test scores. This is an important step, yet much more can be done.

Carter summarizes the concept of outcomes monitoring in a Fall 1984 article in *Public Welfare*. He explains how to measure agency success levels through systematic yet fairly simple steps for monitoring the progress of representative samples of job trainees, children, adults, and families that have been served by state government. This tool ought to be implemented in Illinois. We are flying blind without such outcomes measures.

Back to Old-Fashioned Biennial Budgeting

When I entered the Illinois House of Representatives in 1969 the state had just shifted from biennial (two year) budgets to annual budgeting. I was all for this "reform" that was to strengthen the legislature's ability to budget precisely and to exercise more control over the allocation of resources. How wrong I was.

Budgeting is the formal allocation of money that agencies may spend. The process is central to government, as the allocation of dollars is a reflection of where priorities and values lie. The three Illinois budget books (narrative, appendix, and personnel detail) that the Governor presented to the legislature for its consideration in February 1988 totaled more than 1,150 pages and proposed spending $20+ billion. The Governor's budget was translated later into about 100 appropriations bills; the legislators added about four hundred of their own spending proposals.

The legislative and executive branches have to deal with four separate budget years simultaneously. To illustrate, in June of 1988 the legislature's Auditor General was evaluating how agencies handled funds in the most recent completed year (FY87); the agencies were implementing their FY88 appropriations; the lawmakers were considering FY89 spending requests, and the executive agencies were beginning preparation of their FY90 requests.

Instead of controlling the budget process, legislators and staff have become captives of the consuming *process* of budgeting. Instead of serving as a board of directors that sets broad policy directions for the state, the lawmakers have become clerks who spend too much time cutting a few dollars here and adding them elsewhere.

Agency directors and university heads are unable to plan for the most effective use of scarce resources. Their fiscal year begins July 1, long before final gubernatorial actions and veto override votes are completed in November. At that point it is only eight months to the next fiscal year. So much time is taken in preparing, debating, implementing, and reviewing budgets that none is left to stand back and look ahead a couple of years to anticipate demographic and economic trends. It's crazy.

I propose the governor and legislature return to two-year budgets. The first year of each biennial session could be devoted primarily to budgeting and general legislation. The second year could focus on evaluation of the preceding biennial budget (for which staff analysis could have been completed). I propose also that at the beginning of each four-year gubernatorial term, the executive and legislature engage in "quadrennial (four year) budget mapping." This nonbinding activity would provide state agencies and the education community a sense of where the two branches think the state ought to be headed. This would induce strategic thinking about the best allocations for scarce resources, something that is almost totally absent at present.

The Illinois Constitution of 1970 directs the governor to submit a budget "for the ensuing fiscal year." This would not preclude the chief executive from presenting a two-year budget at the beginning of a biennium, and then proposing minor changes if necessary at the start of the second year.

Illinois Needs to Save for a Rainy Day

Illinois state government rides on a financial roller coaster. As economists would say, we have a highly elastic revenue system. For example, our sales tax applies to discretionary purchases of automobiles and appliances, but as of 1983 we properly exempted necessities such as food and drugs from the tax. As a result, according to University of Illinois economist J. Fred Giertz, "Collections can be expected to rise more rapidly than in the past during expansions and fall faster during recessions."

This roller coaster effect is compounded by the fact that demands for state social services diminish when the economy is expanding and increase when the economy declines. Thus, on the downward slope, there is a double whammy—rapidly falling revenue combined with increased demand for important services.

The severe economic contraction in Illinois in 1982-83 was particularly damaging. It induced severe reductions in the budgets of state regulatory agencies. A state health director suggested this may have contributed to the inability to provide protection against a major outbreak of salmonella that caused sickness among thousands in 1985. There were also mid-year cuts in funding for higher education that made a shambles of planning as well as of efforts to retain star faculty members, many of whom were lured to other states.

Public assistance grant levels were frozen for several years, and real buying power for the poor decreased. Children are the primary beneficiaries of these programs, and it is likely their quality of life suffered. In turn, this may have affected their work in the classroom, where low achievement shames us all. Governor Thompson played down these problems when he campaigned for re-election in 1982 and 1986. Immediately thereafter he called for increased revenues to curtail the damage.

In good economic times increases for education and other services are funded from "natural growth" (see preceding chapter) in state revenues. However, when the business cycle turns downward again, as economic history says it will, we will see "natural contraction" instead of growth. What do we do then?

In 1977 Michigan created a budget stabilization (or rainy day) fund for just such an eventuality, because that state also has a volatile revenue structure. In simplified terms it works this way. If the annual growth rate in personal income, adjusted for inflation, exceeds 2% in any year, deposits are made into the rainy day fund. The amount deposited is the percentage above 2% real growth times general fund revenue for the preceding fiscal year.

If there is a negative adjusted growth rate, the legislature may make withdrawals from the fund to maintain services and balance the budget. This countercyclical fund helped Michigan avert a disaster in the late seventies, according to Bob Kleine, director of that state's Office of Tax Analysis. In 1988, California, New York, and Wyoming dipped into their rainy day funds.

The Fiscal Affairs Committee of the National Conference of State Legislatures recommends a rainy day fund equal to about 5% of a state's general fund budget. This would amount to more than $500 million in Illinois. There should be protections in a rainy day fund to prevent it from becoming a cookie jar that is dipped into for political, rather than economic, reasons. Nor should the law require that expenditures be from the fund when cost-cutting and effective management might achieve the same objectives.

A rainy day fund could discourage excessive spending during expansionary times. There is a tendency in state government for excess revenues either to be spent or to be used for tax relief. Often the tax relief becomes permanent and creates difficulties later during bad economic times. The rainy day fund is a prudent middle course between unwise spending and short-sighted tax relief.

The option to a rainy day fund is to proceed as we have been doing in Illinois, that is, to lurch from year to year, riding the public finance roller coaster. We initiate reforms and expand programs when we are at the crest of the peak, then cut or eliminate them when we hit the downward slope, as we did a few years ago. Illinois should closely examine the rainy day funds in Michigan and 31 other states. We need to tame our public finance roller coaster now, for as state government specialist Steven Gold put it, "When it starts raining, it's too late to set up a fund."

Is Our State Government For Rent?

When I was in the Illinois legislature, a joke went around that our votes weren't for sale, but a few of our colleagues were willing to rent theirs out from time to time. I worry that Illinois state government is under greater pressure than ever to award or "rent" its business to those who fill candidate war chests with huge campaign contributions. Unless preventive measures are taken soon, we could be cruising for a major scandal. Gubernatorial candidates talk openly of the need to raise up to $6 million to fund their campaigns. That is not small change.

The people most vulnerable to appeals for big campaign contributions are those who do—or want to do—business with the state. Construction companies alone contributed half-a-million dollars to Governor Thompson's last campaign. The list of road builders and engineering companies that contributed tends to confirm the understanding among politicos that these companies are expected to make their contributions—of $1,000 to $20,000 and more—on a basis that is roughly proportionate to their shares of state business. For example, McHugh Construction, the McCormick Place general contractor for the convention center in Chicago, contributed $22,000 to the 1982 Thompson campaign. This practice has been going on for decades, under both Democratic and Republican administrations.

I have some indirect experience in these matters. In the early 1980s the head of a small engineering firm came to me. "Jim, we don't seem to be able to get any state business, though we have been submitting what we think are good, competitive bids for some time now. Do you have any suggestions?"

According to my second-hand understanding of the game, I responded, "If you make a campaign contribution of $1,000 or $2,000 and make sure a certain person at the Illinois Department of Transportation is aware of it, I am told it might help."

He did so, and he began to get some business.

Two simple factors are putting increased and dangerous pressures on the relationships between givers and elected officials—campaigns cost more than ever and state government is bigger business than ever. So now, in addition to the construction and road-building companies that have traditionally funded political campaigns, we find major law firms and investment banking houses making annual contributions of $5,000 to $20,000 to gubernatorial campaigns.

For example, in the early 1980s the state of Illinois financed more than one-quarter of all rental housing units constructed in the state each year—through the sale of bonds that were exempt from federal income taxation. The governor's "Build Illinois" program included $1 billion in these bonds for more housing. The problem is that many of the projects were for luxury high-rises of questionable value other than to the developers, contractors, lawyers, and investment bankers who profit handsomely from putting these packages together.

The original stated purpose of the Illinois Housing Development Authority (IHDA) was to increase housing stock for persons of "low and moderate incomes," yet rents in the state-subsidized, luxury high-rises along Chicago's lakefront were to range from $640 a month (for an efficiency apartment) to $2,720 per month. I doubt that many poor folks applied.

The primary beneficiaries are pin-striped business people who do not need government's expensive help. It *is* expensive. The tax-exempt bonds cost the national government millions of dollars annually in lost tax revenue that might otherwise go to reduce the deficit. The housing program looked like an example of a public policy whose original purposes had been subverted from helping poor folks to that of further filling the pockets of the rich. In return, these new beneficiaries help fund campaigns in a way the poor cannot.

From July 1984 through June 1985, a nonelection period, Governor Thompson's political committee raised $1 million. Two-thirds of the total came in amounts of $1,000 or more. I am making an educated estimate that three-quarters of the total came from people and companies that do business with the state or that are affected directly by state regulations.

These contributions are legal and Governor Thompson is an honest man. How then might a scandal be brewing? Because of intense pressures on business people to do business, and on middle-level political appointees in government to raise campaign funds. At some point a quid pro quo—a direct link between a contribution and an award of state business— may be offered and accepted by faceless people who should know better. This might then be found out and reported, following which there would be much finger-pointing as people tried to escape blame. *Voilá*, juicy scandal.

Let us hope this scenario does not occur. I propose several policies to reduce the possibility and to take away incentives that tend to subvert public policies, as in housing.

1. Prohibit companies, firms, and their principals from making contributions to candidates for offices with which they do business. According to the Council on Governmental Ethics Laws, this type of prohibition is already in effect in Ohio and

West Virginia as well as in the province of Quebec, Canada. This would have the additional benefit of reducing the incumbent's advantage in fundraising. It might also encourage more companies to seek state business, secure in the knowledge they would not be under pressure to make contributions in order to keep their business.

2. Extend comparative bidding for state business to include legal, financial and consulting services, and lease-back agreements. A committee of the Illinois Legislative Audit Commission has proposed a new procurement act that would impose similar requirements. At present these services, which cost the state scores of millions of dollars annually, are exempt from formal bid requirements. Awards can be made on the basis of highly subjective factors, possibly including campaign contributions.

3. Adopt partial public financing of election campaigns for statewide offices and state legislative races. This is being done in various forms in 17 other states, as well as in our national presidential elections. This would reduce the pressure on candidate fundraising and make running for office more attractive.

State government budgets and candidate campaign budgets have both been growing. We need to take steps now that would separate the two activities as much as possible, so that public confidence in government will not be shaken in the future by charges that state government is for rent.

A Practical Test for Ethical Decisionmaking

During my service in the Illinois House (1969-72), a colleague and friend was indicted and later convicted for taking bribes. He died in prison, a broken man. Several years later his son was a student at a university where I was teaching. The son looked me up, to learn about his father. "I was just a child when Dad had his problems," said the handsome young man, the spitting image of his father.

"What kind of man was he? Was he a bad man, an evil man?"

I replied that his father was a man of good will, much liked by his colleagues. His father just wasn't thinking. He went along, he did what some others around him were doing; he thought it was the way things had always been done. It was a difficult conversation for me.

I do not presume to know better than the next person what is right or wrong. Nor can I anticipate just what decisions we will be asked to make. I will, however, offer you "Nowlan's Practical Test for Ethical Decisionmaking." I suggest we apply the following steps (or others you devise) before making public decisions:

1. Think! Is there any dimension of this decision that could possibly be illegal? (A reviewer suggested that legality is an elastic term often determined by interpretation. He suggests a more practical test: Think! How would this decision *sound* to a grand jury?)

2. *Never* justify a decision solely on the basis that "this is the way it's always been done." Times and attitudes change.

3. Identify a friend or acquaintance whom you respect for great integrity, who will serve unknowingly as your "second opinion conscience." Ask yourself, "How would (your second opinion) see my decision?" Would he or she think it right?

4. How do you want your children to remember you? "Could this decision conceivably ever affect the way they will remember me?"

Melodramatic? I don't think so. Each year the Gallup organization surveys the public about its perceptions of honesty and ethical standards for a list of occupations. Each year "elected state officials" rank in the bottom rungs, just ahead of used car salesmen. To my mind these perceptions are not justified, yet they reflect the shadow cast on all public servants by the judgment lapses of the few.

The proposals in this chapter on managing are not exhaustive. There are undoubtedly better ones to be offered; on closer examination, one or more of these may be found lacking. The best management techniques will never work without discipline and will on the part of elected officials and their staff. With a combination of solid, common-sense techniques and the will to make them work, Illinois state goverment can make better use of its resources.

Chapter 10

Leadership and Change

Since about 1983 the national media, including particularly the editorial writers and reporters on the *Chicago Tribune*, have been berating us to get serious about educating well the coming generation of workers and to do something about the festering underclass. The policy studies centers that dot the New York-Washington, D.C. corridor have been maintaining a drumbeat of similar messages.

Yet we are not seriously in the process of doing either. Why not?

First, we readers of editorial pages—the "attentive electorate" as we are called by social scientists—represent less than ten percent of the adult population. Second, on fundamental issues that might involve some sacrifice, as in higher taxes, elected officials are actually followers—not leaders—of the larger electorate. There is nothing wrong with listening to the public, of course; that is called democracy.

Unfortunately, there has developed what I call the "tyranny of public opinion," which is characterized by disproportionate influence for the large stratum of uninterested, poorly informed citizens, and by almost slavish sensitivity to this public opinion by elected officials. Opinion polls sample the whole electorate, including the 60 percent or so who are basically uninterested in and uninformed about public issues. Economist Mancur Olson calls these folks "rationally ignorant," because they have concluded that the investment of time and effort necessary to become knowledgeable will have literally no impact on the outcomes of issues. As a pollster confided to me, "We do test a lot of ignorance out there." Elected officials often follow that ignorance.

Elected officials tend to have even greater need today than a generation ago to be re-elected to office, for several reasons. The costs in time and money required to campaign for election have escalated dramatically. When I ran a contested campaign for the legislature in 1968 I spent about $4,000; today it is not unusual to spend $100,000 or more in a campaign for the same post. Prospective gubernatorial candidates talk matter of factly about the need to raise $4-6 million to mount good campaigns.

As a result it seems those who make the commitments of time and money to get involved in politics are becoming, more than ever, professional full-time public officials. This is one reason they have increased their salaries and pension benefits significantly. Many state lawmakers feel a strong need to be re-elected, not just for the salary but for the increased pension benefits that are vested with each additional term in office.

Elected officials tend to evaluate their decisions in terms of marginal political costs and benefits. The question is not whether a majority of voters favor or oppose; instead it is—how many votes could this decision cost me, at the margin of my support base, and how might that affect my forthcoming election campaign.

The campaigns themselves are dominated by 30-second TV spots and "sound-bite" snippets on the evening news. Once I was to be interviewed on a Peoria television station newscast. Before going on I asked the anchor what she was going to ask me. "I want to find out your thoughts on education, jobs, and the economy." Fine, I said. How much time will we have? "Oh, we'll have a *full* two minutes." Two minutes is forever on a half hour newscast; typically one gets a few fleeting seconds to make his points.

New York political media guru Tony Schwarz says it is impossible to convey a complex new idea in 30 seconds, so don't try. Instead, find out what is on the voters' minds, then reach into their heads and relate to those stored concerns with a message that resonates favorably.

The problem is the pollsters ask samples of all the voters what is on their minds, including the 60 percent who are basically uninterested. What concerns most of these folks is rather old news that has seeped onto their field of vision over the years. As a result, we tend to develop our public policies in the wake of the wave of change, rather than on the cusp of the wave. Education is a case in point. State leaders in Illinois did not focus on the issue until after pupil test scores had begun to rise, following a steady decline over 15 years.

I call it the politics of caution; it is anything but the politics of leadership.

In addition, as has been mentioned earlier, there is a general lack of confidence—almost a sense of futility—in government's capacity to make a difference on tough issues like the underclass. And a belief that government activity is so broad and inefficient that by cutting waste we can find the money in the budget to fund any new programs we want. Let me illustrate.

In 1987 and 1988 the governor, the *Chicago Tribune*, and a phalanx of education interest groups led the call in the legislature for a tax increase. They failed each time. During the spring of 1988 my buddy Campbell, whose cartoons you see in this book, and I conducted an informal survey among folks in western Illinois—the butcher, the baker, nurses, retired teachers, farmers: "How do you feel about the proposed tax increase?" The answers were almost all along these lines: "I'm against it. Oh, I suppose education could use more money, but if they really need it they can find it somewhere."

Finally, fundamental change is not likely to show results for years, as in the case of nurturing at-risk two-year-olds into productive adults. "The weakness of politics," says Joseph Bower, "is that it takes strength—either a good organization or high credibility—to argue for delayed gratification. In the contemporary politics of 60-second commercials, there is no such thing as investment. Present costs are too tangible, and future benefits too ephemeral, when compared with painless remedies."

That makes it tough to achieve fundamental change in public policy directions. Niccolo Machiavelli, the Renaissance political adviser, was way ahead of us in understanding this. In his famous tract *The Prince*, he observed: "There is nothing more difficult to arrange, more doubtful of success, and more dangerous to carry through, than to initiate a new order of things... Men are generally incredulous, never really trusting new things unless they have tested them by experience."

Yet fundamental change is possible. For example, our air

and water are cleaner today than in 1970. I was in the Illinois House of Representatives that year, as the national environmental quality movement gathered an irresistible head of steam that easily swept aside all who dared oppose it.

I believe four elements are generally needed to achieve significant change: 1) compelling language to crystallize the problem, 2) deep public concern, 3) perseverance, and 4) leadership.

In *Silent Spring,* Rachel Carson presented a compelling narrative that stimulated massive media visibility that in turn aroused deep public anxiety about our environment. Perseverance was also needed to insure that the change was implemented. I know this from direct experience. My major objective in the legislature in 1969-72 was to achieve a law that required increased reclamation of land strip-mined for coal. The issue was visible in my district because of the scarred land left by stripminers. The issue was also highly technical and involved increased costs for the mining companies. My co-sponsors and I were opposed by associations that represented multi-national energy companies as well as by the several hundred sand, gravel, and limestone quarry companies in Illinois.

Time and persistence were necessary. It is a truism that it is easier to beat a bill in the legislature than to pass one. There are endless gates a chief sponsor must clear with his bill, each of which can bring it down— committee assignment, committee hearings, floor amendments, floor vote; then repeat the process in the second house; conference committee; more floor votes; governor's actions. It took us four years to get a bill that we liked, and it has taken additional years to refine it.

As public issues go, it was rather minor and narrow. Because it was an environmental issue something was likely to pass. So forceful leadership was not required (certainly this junior legislator did not provide it). Leadership was not critical overall to significant environmental policy change because the issue reflected broad, deep public anxiety and because it was relatively painless, that is, it did not appear to require big infusions of new money or any great personal sacrifices from the citizenry.

The change I call for in this book will require both, which means change will be impossible without leadership. What is leadership?

Library shelves are filled with books about leadership. One author has collected 350 definitions of it. Basically leadership represents whatever it takes to get a collective job done that would not get done otherwise. Moshe Czudnowski calls it "a necessary remedy... that can be activated when—for predictable reasons—the collective decision-making process becomes inefficient or nonrational." Irving Kristol says leadership lies in the realization that the status quo is no longer sufficient. Leadership is not so much the exercise of power as of the empowerment of others. That is a tall order when the public lacks trust and is largely unaware of the challenges.

The *Peoria Journal-Star* conducted a telephone call-in poll in 1988 in which the paper asked its readers to register support or opposition for a longer, 11-month school year. While the poll was admittedly unscientific, I was struck that only 15 callers supported the idea while 103 were opposed. This response came after four years of media hullabaloo about the need for education reform, of which a longer school year has been a prominent recommendation. If elected officials continue to follow this kind of opinion, rather than lead us to deeper understanding, then fundamental change will not occur.

Before one can empower others, a person in a position to lead must have transformed himself into a true believer, zealously committed to the goals set forward. Then he or she, whether a governor or a Lee Iacocca-styled business leader, must embark on a public crusade to arouse the general public to a deep concern about our deficiencies.

Our policy analysts have filled a cornucopia with tested ideas, possibly too many. Public officials lull us into a false sense of action and accomplishment with their many pilot projects and modest program initiatives that have reassuring titles such as "business incubators" and "economic innovation centers." As Amitai Etzioni said, "Until there is a sea change in our orientation—a recognition that the party must end, that it is time to pull together as a team—until that happens, no quantity of specific ideas will do."

Strong leadership can achieve fundamental change. Industrialist H. Ross Perot provided more leadership in badgering Texans and their state legislators into important, expensive education reform than had a roomful of Lone Star governors before him. Perot did not do it with ideas and written reports alone. He did it with lots of tough-talking public relations, which ultimately pierced the consciousness of the electorate; with a phalanx of lobbyists, and with serious, persistent arm-twisting and brow-beating of state lawmakers.

Unfortunately, at the moment I do not see any larger-than-life business leaders in Illinois willing and able to take up the cause. Irving Harris and Philip Klutznick are admirable senior business leaders in Chicago who are making major contributions to the world around them; there are others. But they are not the types to lead a crusade with the public.

The task will then fall to our candidates for governor, should they have the skill, creativity, zeal, desire to tackle it. They will have to foreswear the standard incremental, marginal change with which lawmakers feel comfortable. "Make no small plans. They have not the potential to stir the emotions," said Daniel Burnham, 19th century planner of Chicago's visionary park system.

Consciousness Raising

Leadership that empowers people cannot be ordered up as if from a menu. We can make it easier, however, for latent leadership to take hold by making the public environment more supportive and receptive to leadership. For example, we could systematically increase the visibility of our major problems. We have a tendency to hide the unpleasant rather than make it visible.

When I was elected to the legislature in 1968 at age 26, I was invited by the superintendent of the Dixon State School (for the retarded) to pay a visit. The "school" was located only 60 miles from my home, just outside my district. Several times over the years I had driven by the manicured rolling lawn that separated highway travelers from handsome red brick cottage-style buildings in the distance. I had never given the institution a second thought.

Inside, however, the superintendent introduced me to the hideous reality of the snake pits in which we had been cramming our severely and profoundly retarded youngsters. There were 150 children per cottage in the two he led us through, instead of the 40 for which they were designed. Conditions seemed akin to a dungeon from the Dark Ages. My attitudes and understanding were changed forever. (One reviewer of my draft manuscript is a former executive with the Illinois Department of Mental Health. He swears it was common knowledge in the department that the superintendent at the Dixon State School, since retired, purposely kept two cottages in the ghastly conditions I just described, so as to accomplish just the impact I also just described, and to increase appropriations to his institution. I cannot get anyone to confirm this, yet I respect my reviewer. If his recollection is correct, the approach represented an effective yet less than admirable consciousness-raising technique.)

The problems of our ghetto schools and of the underclass are also out of sight and thus out of mind for most of us. They ought not be. I propose that whoever sits as governor take the following steps to bring problems to the public. First, hold regular governor's office appointments in different settings in Illinois. One week it could be a day at Marillac House on the West Side of Chicago, the next week a day at State Community College in East St. Louis, and later a day at a settlement house in the Hispanic community in Little Village on the near southwest side of Chicago. The interest group leaders, businessmen, and media who would typically be on the governor's schedule for that day would have to meet in these out-of-the-way settings.

Second, the governor could commit to volunteer four hours per month to work with the least fortunate among us. For several months the chief executive might tutor poor children at the Robert Taylor Homes on the South Side of Chicago, and then for several months assist in the ward of a mental hospital. This would enhance not only his understanding but also the understanding of the public, who would be brought into the nether world of our forgotten citizens by the newspaper, radio, and television reporters who cover the chief executive. A final benefit would be that of possibly increasing further the amount of volunteer work done by other citizens.

Third, a governor could increase public understanding of our rather invisible state government by using the professional staff of his public information office to develop a monthly one-hour documentary for television that might be called *The Governor's World*. As I envision the program, cameras would follow the governor through much of his regular schedule of strategy sessions with aides, give-and-take with legislative leaders, and trips throughout the state. This professional look inside the governor's world would have to be objective, balanced, and critical, not self-serving. If done well it could have great appeal because state government and politics are about the strong and the weak, the good and the bad, much like the stuff of our popular soap operas.

Encompassing Organizations

Leaders need help in achieving fundamental change. They tend not to get it from organized groups. In our political system, the primary entities for linking the public to the public policy arena are interest groups. There are hundreds of these groups registered to lobby in Illinois, from the powerful Illinois Education Association and Illinois Association of Realtors to the small, highly specialized groups such as the state associations for funeral directors, ambulance operators, and acupuncturists.

These legitimate organizations provide valuable information to the political arena. Common sense tells us the groups' staff members are paid out of hard-earned membership dues to further the narrow objectives of their organizations, not the larger interests of the public. Economist Mancur Olson—who I predict will one day win a Nobel Prize for his work on the logic of interest groups—says individual organizations lack incentives to seek broad societal change, because the costs to an organization of such an effort would generally be greater than the benefits for its own members.

This came home to me in the summer of 1988 when I spoke at a national retreat for lobbyists for colleges and universities. I told them they could increase their stature and respect by reaching beyond their narrow interests to those of poor children. I added that it was ultimately in their direct interest to do so because the consequence would be to increase later the numbers who would enroll in colleges. Some seemed sympathetic but most appeared to agree with the skeptic who said, "Look, our college presidents pay us to bring home their bacon. That is how we are evaluated. We can't afford to get involved in other peoples' battles."

Nor does the sum of the special interests equal the public or general interest. We have seen that in Illinois on the issue of reform of the Chicago public school system. In 1988 lobbyists for the school board, teachers, and principals worked to protect their respective turf. School children rarely came up in the negotiations.

Olson pleads for more "encompassing organizations" to offset the narrow focus of the special interests. The Citizens League of Minneapolis-St. Paul offers a possible model. This is a highly-visible organization that receives support from top business and community leaders as well as from just plain interested citizens. League members engage in well-researched task force studies of major problems facing Minnesota. When Twin Cities chief executives are asked to devote good chunks of their valuable time to chair the task forces, they do so.

After the recommendations have been shaped, the League pushes aggressively inside the political arena for their adoption. They take the recommendations beyond the newspaper opinion pages. They bridge thought to action. And they have a big voice in Minnesota politics.

Illinois has no such encompassing, general interest organizations. The League of Women Voters, which now admits men, has become more activist in recent years, yet lacks the visibility, resources, and influence of the Citizens League. Common Cause of Illinois would like to claim the mantle as the state's encompassing organization, yet it operates on a financial shoe-string and tends to focus on rather narrow process issues such as campaign finance and "sunset" laws. Like the LWV it lacks active participation of business leaders.

The Junior League is another organization that has become more deeply involved in broad social issues in recent decades and has potential to develop resources and influential leadership, but it is also far from the kind of organization that the Citizens League represents in Minnesota. Minnesota is a rather homogeneous state with a strong civic culture that applauds uncompensated participation in public affairs. Illinois is just about the opposite. Nevertheless, Illinois could benefit from the work of a single, respected general interest organization, or from a coalition of groups such as those I cite just above.

154 A NEW GAME PLAN FOR ILLINOIS

SNAKE OIL

No Substitute for Leadership

When all is said and done, fundamental change will not come without leaders who transform our sense of who we are and what we have to do. Where is our shame, our outrage that the equivalent of Third World nations are festering at the edges of our city centers, in plain view from lofty perches in high-rise palaces built for financiers and lawyers?

What has happened to our sense of public service? Is it represented by those state lawmakers who often seem preoccupied with their state pension benefits? By bright young state executives who spin out of public service to make big bucks working for investment banking or law firms that ply state work?

Simply put, we need convince the best among successful business and professional figures—those who should have nothing further to prove to themselves—that they have the responsibility of *noblesse oblige* to call them to the challenges of public leadership. And once enlisted, they must resist the siren calls of the political consultants for whom winning is the only game. Winning alone is *not* enough. With enough money, a wily consultant, and a slick rented campaign operation, just about anybody can win.

The real challenge is to win with compelling purposes clearly stated during the election campaign. That's tougher. But as Teddy Roosevelt said, the credit belongs to the man who is actually in the arena, who "if he fails at least fails while daring greatly."

Nor will the man or woman inside the arena be able to lead if he or she is without benefit of strategic thinking about where we have been and a clear sense of where we ought to be heading.

Strategic Thinking for Illinois

As noted in the Introduction, former North Carolina governor Terry Sanford once lamented, "There is no one in the governor's office whose only job is to gaze out the window and brood about the problems of the future." That is certainly true in Illinois, based on my experience in both the executive and legislative branches of our state government.

Inside government there is neither the time nor the incentive to look ahead. There is always today's health insurance crisis to solve, prison disturbance to quell, natural disaster to ameliorate, and sundry political brush fires to dampen, if possible. The future is never more distant than the next election, which is always visible on the horizon. Why then would any practical politician look beyond?

Nor does there seem to be time for candidates to reflect much on the challenges posed by the posts they seek. Instead, millions of dollars must be raised and higher name recognition achieved, so campaign handlers launch their candidates on a whirlwind of fleeting public appearances up and down the length of Illinois, a state that stretches from the latitude of Portsmouth, New Hamsphire to near that of Portsmouth, Virginia.

"No problem" about the issues, the campaign consultants reassure their candidates. You're only going to talk about the one or two issues of most importance at this moment to most voters, and we'll package your comments into catchy sound bites of 30 seconds or less. In the movie *The Candidate*, Robert Redford spoke for many real life candidates when, during his election night victory, he turned to his campaign consultants and asked blankly, "What do I do now?"

Maybe we ought not expect much more from the political system. By nature its purposes are foremost to broker conflict and to reflect the varied constituency and group needs, not to look ahead, lead, and educate. Alas, we are the lesser for our poor understanding of troubled, rapidly evolving Illinois.

State government is generally less important and less visible to the public than are the affairs of national and local politics. This is definitely the case in Illinois, where not one of Chicago's four major television stations maintains any regular coverage of the state capital in Springfield. Despite this low visibility, even remoteness, state governments will be required to shoulder even heavier burdens and a greater share of governance in America in the future.

This is so for several reasons. The Reagan Administration reduced the flow of national funds to the states. Tax revolts of the 1970s hit hardest at property taxation, the mainstay of local governments, which are creatures of and dependent on the states. And public demands for services are increasing fastest in those functions that are primarily the responsibilities of state and local governments—education, health care, and physical infrastructure.

As touched on in the preceding chapter, Illinois public policymakers have been operating in the past rather than the present, let alone the future. The prime illustrations have been education and economic development. Illinois did not even genuflect toward education reform until years after problems surfaced. In economic development we belatedly joined other states in chasing after high tech miracles like those in Silicon Valley and Route 128 in Massachusetts that got their starts in the 1940s and '50s.

Why did it take so long to get these issues onto the Illinois public policy agenda? In large measure, policymakers in Illinois and other states have selected their issues from those validated by prominent discussion on the opinion pages of the *New York Times, Wall Street Journal,* and *Washington Post.* If you do not see an issue reported and analyzed extensively there, it must not be important. Second, public officials take cues on issues from their pollsters who ask the broad citizenry what one or two issues concern them most. These tend to be issues of the moment at best, not of the future.

Third, most major policy research units and national news organizations have their headquarters along the Washington-New York-Boston corridor. They comprise many of the nation's brightest thinkers. Bright people like to talk to other bright people. The difficulty is that policy problems fester in out-of-the-way communities across the nation. As might have happened with education, a problem may not come to the attention of bright people in the corridor until one of their own is tapped to head a national commission on the topic.

State leaders in Illinois share the blame when a problem like education is years late getting onto the policy agenda. It was ironic to hear a network radio reporter declare that "in the wake of several national studies of education, state legislatures across the nation are responding to the crisis." It is as if state and local officials won't heed what their own education leaders have been saying for years until they see it validated by the priesthood of national opinion leaders.

Illinois is big—would have the world's 14th largest economy if a nation—and ought to be able to think for itself. Illinois and its leaders need to do long-term thinking, to spend time gazing out the window, brooding about the problems of the future. But we don't. When the Illinois Bureau of the Budget was created in 1969 it had a planning unit, but that has atrophied to nothing. Seven years into his governorship, Jim Thompson set up a policy and planning unit in his office (using federal funds initially). This operation soon became caught up in addressing next week's issues rather those of the next decade.

Major state agencies are required by law to publish annual "state plans" but these represent descriptions of existing policies and programs; they do not look ahead. I have read through these plans and the lifeless prose is guaranteed to cure your insomnia. Even the most far-sighted agency-by-agency "plans" would by their nature be quite narrow and limited. As Charles Levesque, a former member of the governor's policy and planning unit, illustrates:

> In spite of the fact that our state is overwhelmingly urban and encompasses one of the world's great cities, Illinois has no real urban policy. There are many state programs that have direct impact on our cities (home rule, enterprise zones, certified cities, grant and loan programs, to name a few) but these are not coordinated and deal only with fragments of the problems and issues that confront our cities.
>
> We need to address the basic questions of what we want our cities to look like. High concentration population centers like Chicago or the sprawl and decentralization characterized by DuPage County? Something in between? What role can the state play in building or rebuilding cities? The questions are endless, the potential significant, the need dramatic, but we're not even asking the questions. This is another one of those areas where we can learn so much from the experiences of other nations.

I am not suggesting we can predict the future. I have in mind less specific thinking, characterized by management expert Peter Drucker simply as, "What do we have to do today to be ready for an uncertain tomorrow." There are resources to help us. Demographic data come to mind, of course. We know now who will be coming into the workforce in a generation. Our scientists are looking into the future every day in their laboratories and have some sense of when new technologies are likely to be close to commercial application. Here are suggestions for increasing our quotient of strategic thinking.

1. Establish a Bureau of International Affairs in the governor's office. Illinois needs to start thinking as if it were almost a nation of the world, as I sense California does. We need to shift our frame of reference for comparisons from the states to the international arena. In a global marketplace, what advantage does Illinois have if its factory workers are more productive than Michigan's but less so than those in Japan and Korea? Where is our comparative advantage if Illinois students score higher on tests than those is New York yet lag behind children in Western Europe?

The Bureau of International Affairs would be charged with recasting our frame of reference. The multi-lingual staff would work with Illinois' seven foreign offices and faculties of international relations and comparative governments at our universities. They would have the following responsibilities:

* Intelligence gathering. The 50 states are not the only laboratories of public policy development. Innovative programs in agriculture, environmental protection, trade promotion, and urban redevelopment have been shaped in the states and provinces of Australia, Brazil, Canada, and West Germany. We ought to assess Sweden's child support tax that is assessed against parents living away from home and West Germany's early sex education programs that apparently contribute to low rates of teen preganancy there.

* Develop comparative yardsticks that show annually how Illinois stacks up against a set of developed and developing nations on economic, education, and quality of life measures. Over time this could help jar us out of our provincial mindset and stimulate us to set loftier goals for our state. Political, economic, and social developments in Kyoto have impact in Illinois just as do those at home in Kankakee. We need to monitor the world closely so that we can develop a strategy for the "international state of Illinois."

2. Strategic thinking teams. Longterm thinking probably has to be carried on away from the day-to-day crush of problems that confront a governor and his staff. Illinois ought to establish independent strategic thinking teams far removed from the corridors of government, whose sole mission would be to think about the problems and potential of Illinois in 2000 and 2020. I

can envision teams organized around the Center for Advanced Study at the University of Illinois in Urbana, the Institute for Public Policy at the University of Chicago, and Eagle's Nest near Oregon, Illinois, the former artists colony that is now Northern Illinois University's retreat campus.

Each team ought be diverse and accomplished, headed by such folks as Dan Alpert, physicist and thinker, of Urbana; Ray Becker, tough-talking, imaginative Peoria builder; Ardis Krainik, general manager of Chicago's Lyric Opera; Don Haider, public finance specialist at Northwestern University, and Jim Krohe, college dropout and intellectual who writes extensively about the environment and natural resources. The Illinois Resources Network, a brain bank of Illinoisans who are expert on every imaginable subject, could be used to identify resource people. Small state grants could be provided each team for research assistance.

There could be annual retreat gatherings at which the teams would come together to react to and build on team members' educated speculations about the future. Their observations and proposals could be disseminated widely and prominently.

3. The Illinois Policy Seminar. This idea is pirated from California. The concept is simple. Identify one or more important issues. Contract with leading thinkers in the area to develop background papers with recommendations. Bring thinkers and their papers together with prominent folks from business, community, journalism, science laboratories, government, and politics to react, argue, and enrich understanding.

This is actually what the University of Illinois used to do with the Illinois Assembly, under the leadership of Professor Samuel K. Gove. Each year a different topic was selected. A quiet retreat setting such as Allerton House was often the site. Participants concluded the three-day sessions by debating and voting on recommendations, that were published. Many of the recommendations later became public policy. The practice has fallen into disuse and ought to be revived.

Strategic or systematic thinking serves several purposes. First, it can lead to clearer understanding of the likely costs and benefits of different options available for problems that we face right now. For example, Oregon has decided not to fund certain expensive, experimental medical operations for citizens who themselves cannot pay; instead it is putting its limited state resources into increased assistance for prenatal and early childhood health care.

We will be doing more of this kind of health care rationing in the future, even though we resist admitting as much. It will be helpful to decisionmakers to know as much as possible about the consequences of expending $10 million in preventive medicine for youngsters versus spending the same amount on a new hospice program for the terminally ill. These types of either-or policy decisions are going to become more frequent as medical care possibilities further outstrip resources avaliable.

Second, long-term thinking can assist us in thinking through productive new relationships among us. As illustration, there are more small children than ever who need care daily while both parents work; there are also more retirees than ever, many of whom long to make a contribution. There are pilot programs underway in which children spend time regularly in retirement centers under the eye of senior citizens. These new intergenerational relationships may lead to new types of "extended families" or mini-communities.

Third, thoughtful discussion now of questions our culture finds difficult to handle, such as the "right-to-die," may make the issues easier for political leaders and the public to approach in a few years when demand for some type of action becomes greater.

Charting the future is an uncertain business at best. Yet strategic thinking could be invaluable to governors, legislators,and business and academic leaders who would prefer to be remembered for vision rather than hindsight.

Chapter 11

Beyond the Margins of Our Mediocrity— A Summary Essay

Illinois can be characterized as the barely average state. Our educational achievement is mediocre at best, and our lack of commitment to poor children is embarrassing.

Half of Chicago's 65 public high schools rank in the bottom one percent of all schools in the nation on achievement test scores. No wonder the system is called the worst in the nation. In 1988 only 6,900 of 112,000 poor children at risk of failure received the early childhood services that our education reformers told us in 1985 were essential.

We appear not to be shamed by this. Clearly we are not outraged; otherwise we would be doing something about it. Everybody who follows public issues knows what we have to do— get poor children close to the same starting line for education as other kids, and get serious about educating our citizenry in superior fashion. Yet we are not serious about doing either.

Instead our policymakers operate at the margins of our mediocrity. Debate is over how to do a better job of doing what we did last year in Illinois, when what we did last year had almost nothing to do with poor children nor with world competitiveness in education.

We talk school reform yet never discuss a longer school day and a longer school year. So we fund 176 short school days per year while in Japan youngsters attend for 240 days. A Japanese high school graduate has had as much classroom time as an American college graduate.

It is as if we are sleepwalking through our decline. In Illinois we reassure ourselves that things aren't so bad, because we seem to be doing as well as Indiana on this measure and we match

Iowa on that one. But the comparisons are irrelevant, for all our states rank at or near the bottom in international comparisons on math achievement.

Elected officials who call themselves leaders slavishly take the pulse of public opinion. Meanwhile the public is busy with family and jobs, and thus most pay little attention to what is going on in the world. Even so, the public is uneasy about the future. Understandably citizens try to protect themselves as best they can, by fighting government and the taxes that cut into their often tight budgets.

Tyrannized by public opinion, elected officials adopt this shortsighted perspective, and the decline continues.

The fundamental issues that will define Illinois in the decades to come are education; the underclass of permanently poor; perceptions by others and by ourselves of who we are and what we are about, and our level of confidence that we can do something about our futures.

These issues are interrelated. I believe they can be addressed by reaching agreement on goals to which we would commit ourselves, and on which we would measure our progress periodically. The goals must be those we believe in. They must take us beyond mediocrity. They must transform our vision of who we are and of what we can accomplish. I propose two:

* That every poor child in Illinois have a full opportunity to get close to the same starting line for formal education as that for typical middle-class youngsters.

* That our elementary and secondary schools become among the best in the world.

Straightforward goals. Goals that we believe in. Goals we once thought we had pretty much achieved. Why not again?

The goals would require investments of both money and individual commitment far beyond present levels. The goals are achievable, albeit breathtaking for a society comfortable with mediocrity. The resources are available, yet not without sacrifice. I estimate we would need to double the rate of our state income tax on individuals, from 2.5 to 5.0 percent, in order to provide early childhood help to every poor child and to extend the school year from 176 to 210 days.

We know enough about what works to act. The results would not come about in the short term, however. I am drawn to the strategies and patience of the riverboat captain who maneuvers great barge trains down the Illinois River. The captain must take new headings early in order to negotiate that next bend in the river, a bend way down there, out of sight on a foggy winter's morning.

We must take new headings now, for a bend in life that is a decade, even a generation away.

Can elected officials afford to await the longterm outcomes, without short-term benefits to show us for our sacrifice? But there are near-term benefits. If we embarked resolutely on a commitment to these goals for our poor children and schools there would be a transformation in the way the world sees us; more important, in the way we see ourselves and what we are all about.

Leaders are needed to shake us from our sleepwalking, to kindle rage within us at how mediocre we have become, to generate a commitment to goals that befit our compact with one another and with our future.

Nor can you and I afford simply to coach and exhort from the sidelines. There are too few out there on the playing field to carry the ball for us.

So while I have proposed a new game plan for Illinois, neither my plan nor yours will be carried out unless there are leaders and followers willing to get onto the field to take us beyond our mediocrity to achieve goals for which we once thought ourselves worthy.

Notes on Important Sources

This book represents an expansion, refinement, updating, and integration of an earlier compilation of newspaper essays I wrote in 1985, published as *Illinois—Problems & Promise*. I also draw heavily on *Inside State Government—A Primer for Illinois Managers* (1982), for which I was a contributor and editor.

The following publications have been especially valuable sources of information and, from time to time, inspiration. I read them regularly and commend them to persons interested in the issues facing Illinois. They are *Chicago Enterprise*, a newsletter published by the Civic Committee of the Commercial Club of Chicago; the *Chicago Sun-Times*; the *Chicago Tribune*; *Crain's Chicago Business*; *First Reading*, a publication of the Illinois General Assembly; the *Illinois Business and Economic Review*, published by the Bureau of Business and Economic Research of the University of Illinois at Urbana; *Illinois Issues*, and *Illinois Times*.

The bibliography that follows represents sources that have been useful for background, citation, and theft of ideas and perspectives.

Bibliography

Books

Philip Abbott. *Seeking Many Inventions: The Idea of Community in America* (U. of Tennessee Press, 1987).

Terry L. Anderson. *Water Crisis: Ending the Policy Drought* (Johns Hopkins Press and Cato Institute, 1983).

Thomas J. Anton. *The Politics of State Expenditure in Illinois* (University of Illinois Press, 1966).

Benjamin Barber. *Strong Democracy: Participatory Politics for a New Age* (University of California Press, 1984).

Brian Barry and Russell Hardin, eds. *Rational Man and Irrational Society?* (Sage, 1982).

Thomas Bender. *Community and Social Change in America* (Johns Hopkins University Press, 1978).

Joseph L. Bower. *The Two Faces of Management* (Houghton Mifflin, 1983).

Samuel Bowles and Herbert Gintis. *Schooling in Capitalist America* (Basic Books, 1976).

Harry C. Boyte. *Community Is Possible: Repairing America's Roots* (Harper and Row, 1984).

Rachel B. Bratt, Chester Hartman, and Ann Meyerson. *Critical Perspectives on Housing* (Temple University Press, 1986).

Severyn T. Bruyn and James Meehan, eds. *Beyond the Market and the State* (Temple University Press, 1987).

James MacGregor Burns. *Leadership* (Harper & Row, 1978).

Thomas C. Cochran. *Social Change in America* (Harper Torchbooks, 1972).

John E. Coons and Stephen D. Sugarman. *Education by Choice* (University of California Press, 1978).

Matthew A. Crenson. *Neighborhood Politics* (Harvard University Press, 1983).
Moshe M. Czudnowski, ed. *Political Elites & Social Change* (Northern Illinois University Press, 1983).
Scott C. Davis. *The World of Patience Gromes* (University Press of Kentucky, 1988).
John Patrick Diggins. *The Lost Soul of American Politics* (Basic, 1984).
Folke Dovring. *Farming for Fuel* (Praeger Publishers, 1988).
David Easton. *A Systems Analysis of Political Life* (Wiley, 1965).
Paulo Freire. *The Politics of Education* (Bergin & Garvey Publishers, Inc., 1985).
Milton & Rose Friedman. *Free To Choose* (Harcourt Brace Jovanovich, 1980).
Benjamin Ginsberg. *The Captive Public* (Basic Books, 1984).
Steven D. Gold, ed. *Reforming State Tax Systems* (National Conference of State Legislatures, 1986).
J.W. Gough. *The Social Contract* (Greenwold, 1978).
Guy Gran. *Development by People: Citizen Construction of a Just World* (Praeger Publishers, 1983).
J. David Greenstone, ed. *Public Values and Private Power in American Politics* (University of Chicago Press, 1982).
Kristen A. Gronbjerg, Madaleine H. Kimmich and Lester M. Salamon. *The Chicago Nonprofit Sector in a Time of Government Retrenchment* (Urban Institute Press, 1985).
Murray L. Gruber. *Yardsticks for Illinois* (Loyola University School of Social Work, Chicago, 1988).
Thomas K. Hammer. *Sources, Characteristics, and Policy Implications of the Urban Underclass* (NCI Research, 1987).
Vivien Hart. *Distrust & Democracy* (Cambridge University Press, 1978).
Paul Hawken. *The Next Economy* (Holt, Rinehart and Winston, 1983).
George Hemmens, et al. *Hardship and Support Systems in Chicago, Vol. 4* (School of Urban Planning, University of Illinois-Chicago, August 1986).
Robert P. Howard. *Mostly Good and Competent Men* (*Illinois Issues* and the Illinois State Historical Society, 1988).
Jane Jacobs, *Cities and the Wealth of Nations* (Random, 1985).
Christopher Jencks. *Who Gets Ahead* (Basic Books, 1979).

William B. Johnston. *Workforce 2000* (Hudson Institute, 1987).
David T. Kearns and Denis P. Doyle. *Winning the Brain Race* (Institute for Contemporary Studies, 1988).
Steven Kelman. *Making Public Policy* (Basic Books, 1987).
Roger L. Kemp, ed. *America's Infrastructure* (Interstate Printers & Publishers, 1986).
James R. Kluegel and Eliot R. Smith. *Beliefs About Inequality* (Aldine de Gruyter, 1986).
Frank Kopecky and Mary Sherman Harris. *Understanding the Illinois Constitution* (Illinois Bar Foundation, 1986).
James Krohe, Jr. *Toxics and Risk (Illinois Issues* and Sangamon State University, 1986).
James Krohe, Jr. *Water Resources in Illinois (Illinois Issues* and Sangamon State University, 1982).
James Krohe, Jr. *Breadbasket or Dust Bowl?* (*Illinois Issues* and Sangamon State University, 1982).
David R. Lampe. *The Massachusetts Miracle* (MIT Press, 1988).
Charles A. Lave, ed. *Urban Transit* (Pacific Institute of Public Policy, 1985).
Jay Mac Leod. *Ain't No Makin' It* (Westview, 1987).
Neil S. Mayer. *Neighborhood Organizations and Community Development* (Urban Institute Press, 1984).
Anna J. Merritt. *Regionalism and Political Community in Illinois* (Institute of Government and Public Affairs of the University of Illinois, 1988).
Claus Mueller. *The Politics of Communication* (Oxford, 1973).
Charles Murray. *Losing Ground* (Basic Books, 1984).
Douglass C. North. *Structure and Change in Economic History* (Norton, 1981).
James D. Nowlan. *Illinois: Problems and Promise* (Illinois Public Policy Press, Galesburg, 1986).
James D. Nowlan. *The Politics of Higher Education* (University of Illinois Press, 1976).
James D. Nowlan, ed. *Inside State Government: A Primer for Agency Managers* (Institute of Government and Public Affairs of the University of Illinois, 1982).
Mancur Olson, Jr. *The Rise and Decline of Nations* (Yale University Press, 1982).
Mancur Olson, Jr. *The Logic of Collective Action* (Harvard University Press, 1983).

Alan Pifer and Lydia Bronte, eds. *Our Aging Society* (Norton, 1986).
Robert Reich. *Tales of a New America* (Times Books, 1987).
A. James Reichley. *Religion in American Public Life* (Brookings, 1985).
Harrell Rodgers. *Poor Women, Poor Families* (Sharpe, 1986).
Walter A. Rosenbaum. *Energy, Politics, and Public Policy* (CQ Press, 1981).
Larry Sabato. *Goodbye to Good-time Charlie: The American Governorship Transformed* (Congressional Quarterly, 1983).
E.S. Savas. *Privatizing the Public Sector* (Chatham House, 1982).
Isabel V. Sawhill, ed. *Challenge to Leadership* (Urban Institute Press, 1988).
William Shirer. *Nightmare Years* (Bantam).
Paul Simon. *Let's Put America Back to Work* (Bonus Books, 1987).
Paul Simon. *The Tongue-Tied American* (Continuum, 1980).
Ted Sizer. *Horace's Compromise: The Dilemma of the American High School* (Houghton Mifflin, 1984).
Thomas Sowell. *A Conflict of Visions* (William Morrow, 1987).
Gregory D. Squires, Larry Bennett, Kathleen McCourt, and Philip Nyden. *Chicago: Race, Class, and the Response to Urban Decline* (Temple University Press, 1987).
Gilbert Y. Steiner. *The Futility of Family Policy* (Brookings, 1981).
Bruce Stokes. *Local Solutions to Global Problems* (Norton, 1981).
Lawrence Susskind, Michael Elliott and Associates. *Paternalism, Conflict, and Co-production: Learning from Citizen Action and Citizen Participation in Western Europe* (Plenum Press, 1983).
Robert Theobald. *Avoiding 1984* (Swallow Press, 1982).
Lester C. Thurow. *Zero Sum Society* (Simon & Schuster, 1980).
Lester C. Thurow. *Zero Sum Solution* (Simon & Schuster, 1985).
Lester C. Thurow. *Dangerous Currents* (Random House, 1983).
John A. Tuccillo. *Housing Finance* (Urban Institute Press, 1983)

Herbert Walberg, et al. *We Can Rescue Our Children* (Heartland Institute, 1988).
Robert H. Walker. *Reform in America* (University Press of Kentucky, 1985).
Norman Walzer and David L. Chicoine. *Financing State and Local Governments in the 1980s* (Oelgeschlager, Gunn & Hain, Publisher, Inc., 1981).
Roy Wehrle. *Economic Development in Illinois* (Illinois Issues andSangamon State University, 1985).
Merry White. *The Japanese Educational Challenge* (The Free Press, 1987).
Martin Wiener. *English Culture and the Decline of the Industrial Spirit 1850-1980* (Cambridge University Press, 1981).
George F. Will. *Statecraft as Soulcraft* (Simon and Schuster, 1983).
William Julius Wilson. *The Truly Disadvantaged* (University of Chicago Press, 1987).

Articles & Papers

Robert P. Abeshouse. "Lifelong Learning Part I: Education for a Competitive Economy," Roosevelt Center for American Policy Studies, Washington, D.C., September 1987.
John W. Ahlen. "Dilemma of Hazardous Waste: Land Disposal," *Illinois Issues*, April 1984.
William H. Allen. "Coal Research Aimed at No. 1 Enemy: Sulfur," *Illinois Issues*, April 1986.
Daniel Alpert. "Industrial Spin-offs from Universities," Center for Advanced Study, University of Illinois, Urbana, 1985.
Karen Baehler. "Lifelong Learning Part II: Training for a Competitive Work Force," Roosevelt Center for American Policy Studies, Washington, D.C., September, 1987.
Karl Leif Bates. "Water Diversion from the Great Lakes," *Illinois Issues*, December 1984.
Jeff Brody. "Budget Cuts to Hurt Productivity," *Illinois State Journal Register*, August 6, 1987.
Casey Bukro. *Chicago Tribune*, p. 8, October 28, 1987.
James W. Carey. "High tech and high ed," *Illinois Issues*, March 1984.

Allan Carlson. "Testimony to the U.S. Taskforce on the Family," Washington, D.C., May 16, 1986.

Cheng H. Chiang and Richard Kolhauser. "Who are we? Illinois' changing population," *Illinois Issues*, December 1982.

Forrest Chisman and Alan Pifer. "Social Spending Can Avert a Recession," *New York Times*, November 22, 1987.

John E. Chubb. "Why the Current Wave of School Reform Will Fail," *Public Interest*, Winter 1988.

Larry Cuban. "You're on the Right Track, David," *Phi Delta Kappan*, April 1, 1988.

Thomas Byrne Edsall. "The Return of Inequality," *The Atlantic Monthly*, June 1988.

Alec M. Gallup and Stanley M Elam. "The 20th Annual Gallup Poll of the Public's Attitudes Toward the Public Schools," *Phi Delta Kappan*, September 1988.

David T. Kearns. "An Education Recovery Plan for America," *Phi Delta Kappan*, April 1988.

Robert J. Kleine and John Shannon. "Characteristics of a Balanced and Moderate State-Local Revenue System," provided to the author by Douglas Whitley, January 1986.

Margaret S. Knoepfle. "Municipal garbage: government goes all out to reduce, recycle it," *Illinois Issues*, August-September 1986.

Margaret S. Knoepfle. "Hazardous wastes: an overview," *Illinois Issues*, November 1983.

Richard Kolhauser. "The Growth in State Taxes: A Review of the 1971-1987 Period," *Illinois Business Review*, June 1988.

James Krohe, Jr. "Mined land reclamation: ends and means," *Illinois Issues*, December 1984.

Charles Levesque. "Building for the Future: Economic Development Opportunites for Community Action Agencies," Illinois Community Action Association, Springfield, Illinois, August 1988.

Dale Mann. "The Honeymoon Is Over," *Phi Delta Kappan*, April 1988.

David Martin. "Wake up: The American Dream is fading, and our future is at risk," *The American School Board Journal*, February 1988.

James A. Mecklenburger. "Neither Schools Nor Photocopiers Are Flawless," *Phi Delta Kappan*, April 1988.

Paul Merrion. "Acid rain limits on Midwest," *Crain's Chicago Business*, October 12, 1987.
John L. Mikesell. "General Sales Tax," *Reforming State Tax Systems*, December 1986.
Thomas G. Mortenson. "The Priorities of State and Local Governments in Illinois," unpublished, March 23, 1984.
James D. Nowlan. "Illinois Party Platforms: An Analysis," Institute of Government and Public Affairs of the University of Illinois, Urbana, 1966.
Brendan OhVallachain. "Sectoral Growth Patterns at the Metropolitan Level," NCI Research, Evanston, Illinois, 1987.
Edward V. Regan. "Government, Inc.: Creating Accountability for Economic Development Programs," Government Finance Officers Association, Washington, D.C., April 1988.
Harold A. Richman and Matthew W. Stagner. "Children in an Aging Society," Chapin Hall Center for Children at the University of Chicago, 1986.
Morris Rosenberg. "Misanthropy and Political Ideology," *American Sociological Review*, December 1956.
Matthew Stagner and Harold Richman. "Help-Seeking and the Use of Social Service Providers by Welfare Families in Chicago," Chapin Hall Center for Children at the University of Chicago, 1986.
T. Paul Torda. "Hazardous waste: the search for solutions," *Illinois Issues*, February 1984.
Barbara Vobedja. "When School Districts Fail," *Washington Post Education Review*, November 1, 1987.
Brian Walden. "Apply the Brakes to Our Local Politicians," *The Sunday Times*, London, July 26, 1987.
"Can America Compete," *Business Week*, April 20, 1987.
"The Great Jobs Mismatch," *U.S. News & World Report*, September 7, 1987.
"Needed: Human Capital," *Business Week*, September 19, 1988.
Business and Education: Focusing on Children-at-Risk. Edna McConnell Clark Foundation Coalition Conference, Chicago, April 1988.
Capital Budgeting and Finance: The Legislative Role, National Conference of State Legislatures, Denver, Colorado, November 1987.

Reports

Alcohol and Drugs in the Public Schools: Implications for School Leaders. National School Boards Association, Washington, D.C., 1988.
Annual Report. Illinois Department of Revenue, 1986 and 1987.
Annual Report 1987. Illinois State Board of Education, Springfield, January 1988.
Barriers to Excellence: Our Children at Risk. National Coalition of Advocates for Students, Boston, Massachusetts, 1985.
A Blueprint for Success. National Foundation for the Improvement of Education, Washington, D.C., 1987.
Brent Bohlen. *Illinois Tax Climate*, Taxpayers' Federation of Illinois, Springfield, 1987.
Bringing Down the Barriers. National Governors' Association, Washington, D.C., 1987.
William R. Bryan, Robert W. Resek, and Alice K. Waldoff. *1987 Illinois Economic Outlook*, Bureau of Economic and Business Research, University of Illinois, Urbana, 1987.
Roland W. Burris, Comptroller, State of Illinois. *Long-term bonded indebtedness shows dramatic increase: Illinois still ranks last in return of federal funds*, Springfield, May 1, 1987.
Roland W. Burris. *State of Illinois Fiscal Condition Report*, Comptroller, State of Illinois, Springfield, December 31, 1987.
Roland W. Burris. *State of Illinois Fiscal Condition Report*, Comptroller, State of Illinois, Springfield, January 29, 1988.
Roland W. Burris. *State of Illinois Fiscal Condition Report*, Comptroller, State of Illlinois, Springfield, February 29, 1988.
Roland W. Burris. *State of Illinois Fiscal Condition Report*, Comptroller, State of Illlinois, Springfield, March 30, 1988.
David L. Chicoine and J. Fred Giertz. *Property Tax Assesssment in Illinois: Structure and Performance*, Illinois Tax Foundation, Springfield, December 1986.
Children in Need. Committee for Economic Development, New York, 1987.

A Children's Agenda, 1988. Voices for Illinois Children, Chicago, 1988.

Comparison of Fiscal Disparity. Minnesota Department of Revenue, St. Paul, 1987.

Daring Goals for a Caring Society, Independent Sector, Washington, D.C., 1986.

Data Report. Illinois Department of Children and Family Services, Springfield, 1986 and 1987.

Division of Youth and Community Services: Overview of Administration and Programs, Illinois Department of Children and Family Services, Springfield, January 1987.

Randy Erford. *Illinois State Spending: The Thompson Years,* Taxpayers' Federation of Illinois, Springfield, 1988.

Deborah L. Fields. *Cogeneration Market Assessment,* Illinois Department of Energy and Natural Resources, Springfield, October 1987.

First Reading. Illinois General Assembly Legislative Research Unit, quarterly, August 1988.

Fiscal Year 1989 Economic Outlook and Revenue Estimate Update. State of Illinois Economic and Fiscal Commission, Springfield, November 16, 1988.

Tor Ragnar Geerholm & Herman Kahn. *What about the Future?,* Hudson Institute and KREAB Development, Indianapolis 1984.

General Funds Revenue: Fiscal Year 1971 through Fiscal Year 1987. Illinois Economic and Fiscal Commission, Springfield, April 1988.

Thomas R. Hammer. *Sources, Characteristics, and Policy Implications of the Urban Underclass,* NCI Research, Evanston, Illinois, September 1986.

George Hemmens, Charles Hock, Donna Hardina, RoJean Madsen, and Wim Wiewel. *Changing Needs and Social Services in Three Chicago Communities,* School of Urban Planning and Policy, the U. of Illinois at Chicago, August 1986.

Leonard F. Heumann. *Illinois Housing,* Housing Research and Development Program, U. of I. at Urbana, November 1984.

Highlights of FY 1988 Revenue Update and Preliminary FY 1989 Revenue Outlook. State of Illinois Economic and Fiscal Commission, Springfield, February 19, 1988.

Harold C. Hodgkinson. *Illinois: the State and its Educational System*, The Institute for Educational Leadership, Inc., Washington, D.C. 1989

Harold L. Hodgkinson. *All One System: Demographics of Education—Kindergarten Through Graduate School*, Institute for Educational Leadership, Washington, D.C., 1985.

Illinois 1999: The Successful Center, unpublished, Office of the Governor, State of Illinoiis, Springfield, 1987.

Illinois State Budget. Office of the Governor, Springfield 1985-89.

Illinois: Jobs for the Future. Department of Commerce and Community Affairs, Springfield, 1985.

Curtis C. McKnight, F. Joe Crosswhite, John A. Dossey, Edward Kifer, Jane O. Swafford, Kenneth J. Travers, Thomas J. Cooney. *The Underachieving Curriculum: Assessing U.S. School Mathematics From an International Perspective*, International Association for the Evaluation of Education Assessment, Urbana, Illinois, January 1987.

Measuring State Fiscal Capacity, 1987 edition. Advisory Commission on Intergovernmental Relations, Washington, D.C., December 1987.

Metropolitan Tax Base Sharing: An Introduction to Minnesota's Fiscal Disparities Law. Research Department of the Minnnesota House of Representatives, St. Paul, August 1984.

Monthly Fiscal Report, Comptroller, State of Illinois, Springfield, October 1987.

Thomas Mortenson. *Notes of the Changing Human Capital Needs of Illinois*. Illinois State Scholarship Commission, Springfield, 1983.

Thomas Mortenson. *Teenage unemployment rates in Illinois by race and region*. Illinois State Scholarship Commission, Springfield, July 1986.

Peter F. Nardulli and Michail Krassa. *Regional Animosities in Illinois: An Overview and an Assessment*, Institute of Government and Public Affairs of the University of Illlinois, Urbana, 1987.

R. Dan Neely and Carla G. Heister. *The Natural Resources of Illinois*, Illinois Natural History Survey, Department of Natural Resources, State of Illinois, Springfield.

F. Howard Nelson. *Implementing Educational Reform*, Chicago Panel on Public on Public School Finances, November 1985.

New Horizons in Long Term Care. Illinois Department of Public Aid, Springfield, undated.

Our Future at Risk. Joint Committee on Minority Student Achievement, State Board of Education and Illinois Board of Higher Education, Springfield, April 1988.

Performance Profiles: Illinois Schools Report to the Public, Illinois State Board of Education, Springfield, May 1987.

Public Policy on Mental Illness in Illinois. Mental Health Task Force, League of Women Voters of Illinois Education Fund, Chicago, 1986.

Report of Recommendations to the 84th Illinois General Assembly. Joint Committee on Public Utility Regulation, Springfield, April 1985.

Revenue Estimate and Economic Outlook. Illinois Economic and Fiscal Commission, Springfield, 1989.

Gregory L. Rhodes and Mark Real. *Day Care: Investing in Ohio's Children*, Children's Defense Fund, Washington, D.C., 1985

Audrey M. Ryack. *Breach of Contract? Some Contemporary Work Dilemmas and the American Social Contract on Work*, Roosevelt Center, Washington, D.C., August 1984.

Schools That Work. U.S. Department of Education, Washington, D.C.

Isaac Shapiro and Robert Greenstein. *Holes in the Safety Nets: Poverty Programs and Policies in the States*. Center on Budget and Policy Priorities, Washington, D.C., April 1988.

Isaac Shapiro aand Robert Greenstein. *Illinois: Holes in the Safety Nets: Poverty Programs and Policies in the States*, Center on Budget Policy Priorities, Washington, D.C., Spring 1988.

Significant Features of Fiscal Federalism, 1988 Edition, Volume II, Advisory Commission on Intergovernmental Relations, Washington, D.C., December 1987.

Significant Features of Fiscal Federalism, 1988 Edition, Volume I. Advisory Commission on Intergovernmental Relations, Washington, D.C., July 1988.

Social Indicators of Equality for Minorities and Women. United States Commission on Civil Rights, Washington, D.C., August 1978.

State Budget Actions in 1987. National Conference of State Legislatures, Denver, Colorado, August 1987.

State, Local, and Federal Financing for Illinois Public Schools 1986-1987. Illinois State Board of Education, Springfield, January 1987.

Summary of Fiscal Year 1989 Appropriations for Higher Education Operations and Grants. 85th General Assembly, State of Illinois, Springfield, Illinois, July 1, 1988.

Tax Facts. Taxpayers' Federation of Illinois, Springfield, 1987.

Mark Testa and Edward Lawlor. *The State of the Child: 1985,* Chapin Hall Center for Children at the University of Chicago, 1985.

The Budding Revolution in State Income Taxes. National Conference of State Legislatures, Denver, Colorado, December 1987.

The First Sixty Months. National Governors' Associationn Committee on Human Resources and Center for Policy Research, Washington, D.C., July 1987.

Theatre Chicago. League of Chicago Theatres, Chicago, 1987.

Time for Results: The Govenors' 1991 Report on Education. National Govenors' Association, Washington, D.C., August 1986.

The Fourth R: Workforce Readiness. National Alliance of Business, Washington, D.C., 1987.

Learning Outcomes for College-Bound Students and Public University Admission Requirements. State of Illinois Board of Higher Education, Springfield, October 6, 1987.

A Working Paper on the Future of Illinois. Task Force on the Future of Illinois, State of Illinois, Springfield, January 1979.

Index

Abbott, Philip, 24
Addams, Jane, 88
Aid to Families with Dependent Children, 82, 87
Alexander County, 11
Alexander Grant (an accounting firm), 102
Alpert, Daniel, 68-69, 73, 160
Alsberg, Pete, 68
Alumni Panels on University Cost Effectiveness, 75
American Assembly, 74
American College Testing (ACT) scores, 39, 48
American College Testing Program, 118
Amoco Oil of Chicago, 14, 64
Amtrak's Illinois Zephyr, 103
Anderson, Betty, 89
Anderson, Terry L., 105
Anton, Thomas J., 112
Arkansas, 83
Atlantic Monthly, 81
Auditor General, 113, 137
Australia, 10

Barrington, 48
Beck, Joan, 36
Becker, Ray, 160
Beckman Institute, 69
Beckman, Arnold, 69

Beethoven Elementary School, 86
Beethoven Project, 86
Beethoven Satellite Network, 97
Belleville, 22, 59
Bennett, William, 47
Biennial budgeting, 136-138
Biodegradable plastics, 64
Biotechnology Research and Development Consortium, 63-64
Biotechnology, 64
Black Hawk Community College at Kewanee, 65
Bloom, Benjamin, 37
Bloomington, 12, 97
Boston, 95
Bower, Joseph, 147
Brady, Ron, 67
Brann, Lester, 118
Bridgeport (Chicago neighborhood), 24
Brown, William, 70
Budgeting, 111-117
"Build Illinois", 62, 141
Bureau of International Affairs, 159
Bureau of the Budget, 130, 135, 158
Bureau of the Census, 96
Bureaucracy, 133-135
Bush, George, 71

Cabrini-Green, 80-81
Caldwell, Lynton, 105
California, 60, 63, 70, 96, 102, 139, 159
Campbell, Bill, 30
Canada, 59
Carey, James W., 71
Carlson, Richard J., 105
Carnegie, Andrew, 29
Carson, Rachel, 148
Carter, Reginald, 135-136
Caterpillar, 12
Catholic Charities of Illinois, 25, 27
Catholic Diocese of Davenport, 89
Catholic schools, 49
Cedarhurst Chamber Music Series, 97
Center for Advanced Study, 68, 160
Center for Supercomputing Research and Development, 69
Central Illinois Light Company, 64
Central Illinois, 9
Central-western Illinois, 99, 107
Challenge for Higher Education, 71
Champaign-Urbana, 97
Chancellor, John, 19
Changing Faces of Illinois, 8-10
Chapin Hall Center for Children, 23
Charleston (Illinois), 9
Chester, 5
Chiang, Cheng H., 8
Chicago Art Exposition, 96
Chicago Board of Education, 80
Chicago businesses, 43
Chicago International Theatre Festival, 96
Chicago Panel on Public School Finances, 44
Chicago public schools, 7, 37, 40, 43, 47-50, 77, 153, 163
Chicago School Board, 38, 40, 48
Chicago Teachers' Union, 48
Chicago Tribune, *20, 31, 39, 53, 79, 81, 94, 145, 147*
Chicago White Sox, 34
Chicago's River North district, 96
Chicago's South Side, 80, 151
Chicago's West Side, 22, 38, 79, 151
Child welfare, 27
Children at risk of failure, 43-44, 73, 120, 121
Choice in education, 50
Chrysler-Mitsubishi auto plant, 58
Chubb, John, 45
Cipollone, Rose, 21
Citizen responsibility, 20
Citizens League of Minneapolis-St. Paul, 153
Civil Administrative Code, 14
Civil rights movement, 81
Class of '99, 13, 14, 16
Coal, 64, 98-99
Coleman, James, 23
Comiskey Park, 6
Commercial Club of Chicago, 94
Commission on Economy and Efficiency, 128
Committee for Economic Development, 83
Common Cause of Illinois, 153
Community colleges, 51, 54
Competitiveness, 57
Comprehensive community aid formula, 28
Comptroller, 113
Consciousness raising, 150-152
Conservation Foundation, 100
Cook County, 10, 31

Coons, John, 52
Corn, 99, 100, 103
Corporate/Community School, 43
Council on Governmental Ethics Laws, 142
County poor farm, 29
Creative people, 95-98
Creativity, 58
Critical mass, 64, 69, 70, 76
Czudnowski, Moshe, 149

Dalzell, 5
Democratic Party, 6
Demography, 114
Department of Aging, 14
Department of Agriculture, 100
Department of Children and Family Services, 84
Department of Commerce and Community Affairs, 62
Department of Conservation, 15
Department of Corrections, 13, 14
Department of Employment Security, 11
Department of Financial Institutions, 14
Department of Mental Health and Developmental Disabilities, 14, 27, 151
Department of Nuclear Safety, 14
Department of Public Aid, 14, 25, 26, 27
DeVry Institute of Technology, 51
Diamond Star Chrysler-Mitsubishi auto plant, 12, 58
District of Columbia, 70
Dixon State School, 150-151
Douglas, Stephen A., 9
Dow Chemical, 64
Drake Hotel, 24

Drucker, Peter, 158
DuPage County, 10, 11, 31, 158

Eagle's Nest, 160
Early childhood education, 2, 38
East Germany, 10
East St. Louis public high schools, 13
East St. Louis, 22, 31, 33, 34, 36, 37, 40, 78, 83, 88, 151
Economic development agencies, 58, 108
Economic development, 57, 66
Edgar, Jim, 15
Education achievement, 60
Education Commission of the States, 46
Education Digest, 52
Education reform, 2, 36, 38, 41, 73, 121-122, 150
Education, 3; Chicago public schools, 7, 37, 40, 43, 47-50, 77, 153, 163; early childhood education, 2; early childhood programs, 38; education reform, 2, 36, 38, 41, 73, 121-122, 150; equal at the starting line for formal education, 36, 164; public high schools, 12; public high school students, 35; school mandates, 30, 35, 45, 121; school math, 35;
Edwardsville (Illinois), 7
Elementary and secondary schools, 66, 164
Encompassing organizations, 152-153
Entrepreneurial culture, 61
Entrepreneurs, 67-69
Environmental Consensus Forum, 106
Environmental issues, 98-107

Equal at the starting line for formal education, 36, 164
Espenshade, Thomas, 42
Ethics in government, 140-144
Etzioni, Amitai, 149
Europe, 55
Evanston, 39
Executive training, 134

Fairview Heights, 22
Fine arts, 93-98
Fletcher, James, 1
Florida, 102, 123
Focus on the next generation, 37-38
Food for Century III, 67
Food stamps, 89
Forbes, 136
Foreign language instruction, 54-56
Foreign languages, 4
France, 55
Frank, Jim, 100
Fundamental Government, 28-32

G.I. Bill, 51
Galesburg, 9, 128
Galesburg Register-Mail, 30
Gallup organization, 144
Gallup Survey, 108
Galston, Bill, 108
Garreau, Henry, 24
Gautreaux program, 88
General Motors Saturn plant, 58
General Motors, 128
General Revenue Fund, 25
Geneva, Switzerland, 33
Ghetto Resettlement Program, 88
Giertz, J. Fred, 138
Gold, Steven, 140

Goodman Theatre, 97
Gove, Samuel K., 160
Governing, 96
Governor's James Dunn Fellow Program, 135
Governor's Office of Volunteer Assistance, 22
Governor's office, 128-131
Great Lakes, 60
Groundwater supplies, 104-106
Gruber, Murray, 16, 17
Guadalajara, 80

Haider, Don, 160
Hale, David, 57
Hammer, Thomas, 77
Harris, Irving, 86, 150
Hart, Peter, 6
Hazardous wastes, 102-103
Head Start, 33, 38
Heileman Brewing Company, 59
Henry County, 98
Henry Horner Homes, 79
Heritage Foundation, 50
High school graduation rates, 77
High tech centers, 63
High tech companies, 67
Higher education and economic development, 65-71
Higher education report cards, 75
Higher education, 7, 72, 138; public and private colleges, 22; public universities, 54, 56, 65-71
Hispanics, 9
Hmong tribesmen, 88
Hodgkinson, Harold L., 78
Hogan, John, 119
Hoover Center, 50
Huiskamp, Sister Julia, 90
Hull House, 88

185

Iacocca, Lee, 127, 149
Illinois Association of Realtors, 152
Illinois Board of Higher Education, 67
Illinois Business Review, 117, 119
Illinois Constitution, 138
Illinois demography, 8
Illinois Economic and Fiscal Commission, 115
Illinois economic outlook, 59
Illinois economy, 10
Illinois Education Association, 39, 152
Illinois Environmental Protection Agency, 100
Illinois Farm Bureau, 11, 103, 109-110
Illinois General Assembly, 43, 120
Illinois House of Representatives, 7, 148
Illinois Housing Development Authority, 142
Illinois Institute of Technology, 65
Illinois International, 97
Illinois Issues, 59, 99
Illinois Legislative Audit Commission, 143
Illinois Math and Science Academy, 44
Illinois Natural History Survey, 100
Illinois Policy Seminar, 160
Illinois Resources Network, 160
Illinois River, 60
Illinois State Board of Education, 39, 114
Illinois State Chamber of Commerce, 118-119
Illinois State Scholarship Commission, 74
Illinois State Scholarship Program, 51, 54
Illinois state government, 14-16
Illinois Supreme Court, 15, 20
Illinois tax burden, 116
Illinois' response to economic change, 62-65
Illinois, 100
Illinois--high tax or low tax state?, 117-118
Import replacement goods, 58
Income tax, 39, 164
Independent Sector, 21, 22
India, 10
Indiana Center for Innovation Development, 67
Indiana, 7, 59
Institute for Illinois, 70
Institute for Public Policy, 160
Institute of Government and Public Affairs, 8
Internal Revenue Service, 25
International Harvester, 12
International Mineral and Chemical Corporation, 64

Jacobs, Jane, 57, 58, 94
Japan, 2, 40, 45, 47, 59, 66, 120, 121, 163
Japanese Economic Council, 41
Jencks, Christopher, 41
Jewish Federation, 25
John Hancock Building, 24
Johnson, Gordon, 19, 23
Junior League, 153

Kansas, 99
Kean, Thomas H., 47
Kearns, David, 41
Kenosha, Wisconsin, 128
Kewanee, 5
Kleine, Bob, 139

Klutznick, Philip, 150
Knox College, 48, 65, 100, 111
Kolhauser, Richard, 8, 117
Krainik, Ardis, 160
Krannert Center for the Performing Arts, 96
Kristol, Irving, 149
Krohe, James Jr., 19, 99-107, 160

Ladd, 5
Lake County, 10
Lake Michigan, 100, 101
Lampe, David R., 60
Lane, Mike, 13
Lang, Eugene, 34
Leadership, 109, 147-150, 165
League of Women Voters, 153
Legislative Staff Internship Program, 135
Lemann, Nicholas, 80-82, 88
Lincoln Tutors, 22
Lincoln, 128
Lincoln, Abraham, 8, 9
Lippmann, Walter, 94
Little Village (Hispanic community in Chicago), 24, 151
Locke, John, 29
Lowden, Frank O., 14, 128

Machiavelli, Niccolo, 147
Magid, Ken, 38
Magnet schools, 48
Management by outcomes, 135-136
Management exchanges, 134
Manhattan Institute, 50
Marillac House, 22, 38, 151
Market Opinion Research, 8
Maryland, 70
Massachusetts Institute of Technology, 63, 65, 68

Massachusetts, 2, 63, 70, 157
Mayflower Compact, 33
McCormick Place, 140
McDonald's, 14
McDonald, Jess, 23, 26
McGuiness, Aimes, 46
McHugh Construction, 140
Median family income by educational attainment, 42
Medicaid, 20, 113
Medical assistance green card, 89
Memphis (Tennessee), 6
Mental Health Task Force, 27
Mexico City, 80
Mexico, 10
Michel, Robert H., 64
Michigan Research Corporation, 67
Michigan, 62, 139
Midwest, 59
Mikesell, John, 122
Mill, J.S., 35
Minneapolis, 53, 61, 93
Minnesota, 52, 54, 153
Minorities, 9
Mississippi River, 60, 100
Mitchell Museum, 97
Moline, 9, 12
Morrill Land Grant Act, 29, 66
Morrill Plots, 66
Mortenson, Thomas, 118, 122
Moynihan, Daniel Patrick, 82
Mt. Vernon, 97

Naperstek, Arthur, 23
Naperville, 10
National Center for Supercomputing Applications, 69
National Conference of State Legislatures, 139
National Governors' Association, 2, 83, 134

National Science Foundation, 66
Natural resources, stewardship of, 98-107
NCI Research, 61
Nevada, 125
New Hampshire, 51, 125
New Music Chicago Festival, 96
New York City, 34
New York Telephone Company, 42
New York Times, 43, 103, 157
New York, 96, 139
Nonoperating school districts, 52
Nonprofit groups, 25
North Lawndale, 43
Northern Illinois University, 73-74, 160
Northern Regional Research Center, 63, 108
Northwest Ordinance, 29
Northwest Territory, 24
Northwestern University, 61, 65, 88

O'Hare Airport, 5
Oak Brook, 31
Oak Park, 79
Office of Technology Development, 61
Ogden-Millard Center, 38
Ogilvie, Richard B., 78, 131, 134
Ohio River, 60, 100
Ohio, 142
OhVallachain, Brendan, 61
Olson, Mancur, 57, 145, 152-153
One Church, One Child adoption program, 25, 88
Options for the underclass, 83-91
Oregon (Illinois), 160
Oregon, 160
Ottawa (Illinois), 9

Pacific Rim, 55
Patronage, 131

Pei, Mario, 57
Pennsylvania, 59
People's Republic of China, 62
Peoria Journal-Star, 72, 149
Peoria, 9, 12, 25, 27
Percy, Charles, 6
Pericles, 35
Perot, H. Ross, 149
Perpich, Rudy, 53, 62
Perry Preschool Project, 34, 38
Personal responsibility, 23
Peterson, James E., 61
Pike County, 11
Pittsburgh, 93-94
Plains states, 101
Poitier, Sidney, 5
Poland, 5
Port Huron Statement, 34
Portsmouth, New Hampshire, 5, 156
Portsmouth, Virginia, 5, 156
Prime farmland, 99
Princen, L. H., 64, 108
Prisons, 114
Private colleges, 54, 65
Private schools, 49, 51
Procter and Gamble, 14
Productivity and education, 41-56
Property taxes, 115
Proposals for tax increases and changes, 124
Provincial distrust, 6
Public and private colleges, 22
Public colleges, 54
Public high school students, 35
Public high schools, 12
Public universities, 56, 65-71
Public welfare, 23
Pulaski County, 11

"Quadrennial budget mapping," 138
Quality of life, 93-110

"Rainy day fund," 138
Rand Center, 28, 93
Raspberry, William, 45
Reagan Administration, 156
Reagan, Ronald, 50
Redford, Robert, 156
Reich, Robert, 35
Reilly, Jim, 26
Reorganization of the governor's office, 128-131
Republican Party, 6
Research and development, 69
Rhodes Scholars, 134
Robert Taylor Homes, 11, 86, 151
Rock Falls, 5
Rock Island, 12
Rock Valley Community College, 65
Rockford, 65
Rockwell Gardens, 81
Role of community, 23-28
Roosevelt, Theodore, 154
Rousseau, Jean-Jacques, 29, 33
Rural caucus, 110
Rural Illinois, 9, 11
Rural issues, 107-110
Rural schools, 108-109
Russia, 62

Salganik, Laura H., 52
Salmonella, 104
San Francisco, 95
Sanford, Terry, 1, 155
Saudi Arabia, 60
Schaumburg, 10
School calendar, 121, 163
School Code, 44
School mandates, 30, 35, 45, 121
School math, 35
School Report Card, 136
Schwarz, Tony, 146
Sears, Roebuck and Co., 14

Set-asides, 70
Shakespeare Festival at Ewing Manor, Bloomington, Illinois, 97
Shields, Roger, 97
Shirer, William, 37
Silicon Valley, 61, 157
Simon, Paul, 55
Small Business Innovation Research, 70
Small towns, 24
Smith, Adam, 50, 52
Social compact, 35
Social contract, 33
Southern Illinois University, 7
Southern Illinois, 5, 6, 10
Southwestern states, 101
Soybeans, 99, 103
Spain, 10
Spanish-American War Veterans Commission, 113
Sparta, Illinois, 5
Springfield, 15
Spuller, Alice, 89
Squires, Gregory, 11
St. Louis, 7
St. Paul, 93
Standard of Need, 87
Stanford University, 63, 68
Stark County, 9
State Community College of East St. Louis, 78, 151
"State management draft," 134
State of Illinois Center, 15
State revenue, 114-115
State spending, 113-117
State taxations, 117-126
Steiger, Rod, 5
Steppenwolf Theatre, 97
Strategic thinking, 155-161
Stravinsky International Music Awards, 97
Sugarman, Stephen, 52
Sun Belt states, 101

Sunday Times of London, 30
Super conductor, super collider project, 71
Super Slurper, 63-64
Surface-mined reclamation act, 98-99
Synthetic fuels, 101

Talmadge, John, 61
Tax capacity and tax revenue in Illinois, 119
Tennessee, 58
Texas, 60, 71, 99, 102, 107
"The Governor's World," 151
Thompson, James R., 1, 12, 14, 15, 22, 26, 39, 58, 62, 67, 71, 101, 112, 113, 114, 120, 122, 123, 131, 132, 133, 139, 140, 142, 158
Thurow, Lester, 37, 73
Titmus, Richard M., 19
Topsoil, 100
Toulon Municipal Band, 29
Toulon, 78
Tourism, 62
Toxic chemicals, 102-105
Treasurer, 113
"Tyranny of public opinion," 145, 164

U.S. Advisory Commission on Intergovernmental Relations, 117-118
U.S. Department of Agriculture, 63, 64
U.S. Department of Health and Human Services, 22
U.S. Department of Housing and Urban Development, 22
U.S. Department of State, 89
U.S. News and World Report, 72
U.S. Occupational Safety and Health Administration, 104-105
U.S. Office on Smoking and Health, 21
Underclass ghettos, 89
Underclass, 3, 4, 77-78, 79, 87, 151
Undergraduate teaching, 73
United Kingdom, 30
United Way, 26
University of Calgary Entrepreneurship Institute, 67
University of Chicago, 23, 65, 80, 160; Chapin Hall Center for Children, 23
University of Geneva, 33
University of Illinois, 7, 8, 25, 26, 56, 60, 61, 65, 65-72, 66, 69, 73-74, 96, 103, 160; Biotechnology Research and Development Consortium, 63-64; Center for Advanced Study, 68, 160; College of Liberal Arts, 74; Institute of Government and Public Affairs, 8; Office of Technology Development, 61; School of Public Health, 106
University of Michigan, 70
University of Minnesota, 53
University of Queensland Venture Fund, 67
Urban Institute, 42
Urban League, 2
Urbanek, Dave, 15

Venture capital firms, 60
Venture capitalists, 61
Vermont, 51
Virginia, 70
Voice of Illinois, 97
Voices for Illinois Children, 123

Volkswagen, 59
Volunteer activity, 21; Lincoln Tutors, 22
Vouchers, 50

Wabash, 100
Walberg, Herbert, 49
Walker, Dan, 131, 133
Wall Street Journal, 29, 53, 72, 79, 157
War on Poverty, 81
Washington County, 103
Washington Post, 157
Washington, State of, 83
Washington-New York-Boston corridor, 157
Water, 100-106
Wattenberg, Ben, 77
Wehrle, Roy, 59
Weiner, Martin, 57
Welfare, 85
West Germany, 45
Western Illinois, 10, 11
WFMT radio, 97
White House Fellows, 134
Will, George, 35-36
Wilmette, 37
Wilson, William Julius, 80-83
Wisconsin Child Support Assurance Program, 86
Wisconsin, 7, 86, 132
Wisdom Bridge Theatre, 97
Woodlawn area of Chicago, 88
Woodson, Robert, 24
Wrigley Field, 6
Wyoming (Illinois), 11, 107
Wyoming, 139

Ypsilanti, Michigan, 38